To Drew & Evi
Don't forg'

Much love,
Lisa, Martin, Melanie
& Kirsty x x x
x

Vegan Cookbook for Beginners

Vegan Cookbook for Beginners

THE ESSENTIAL VEGAN
COOKBOOK TO GET STARTED

ROCKRIDGE
PRESS

For general information on our other products and services or to obtain technical support, please contact our Customer Care Department within the U.S. at (866) 744-2665, or outside the U.S. at (510) 253-0500.

Rockridge Press publishes its books in a variety of electronic and print formats. Some content that appears in print may not be available in electronic books, and vice versa.

Front cover photography © Ian Garlick/Stockfood; Back cover photography © Gillian van Niekerk/ Stocksy and Ina Peters/Stocksy

ISBN Print 978-1-62315-230-7 | eBook 978-1-62315-231-4

Contents

PART ONE

Making the Move to Veganism

Introduction

What is it about "going vegan" that has athletes, celebrities, and millions of others around the world raving about their animal-product-free lifestyle? Olympic athlete Carl Lewis has been quoted saying, "My best year of track competition was the first year I ate a vegan diet." Bob Harper, physical trainer who appears in *The Biggest Loser* television show, said, "My cholesterol dropped over 100 points within a month . . . . I feel like there is a fountain of youth attached to living a vegan lifestyle." The benefits of living a vegan lifestyle are many, and the motivations for switching to a vegan diet are as numerous as these benefits.

Veganism is the practice of abstaining from the use and consumption of animal products, including meat, eggs, dairy, and other products derived from animal sources. For some, becoming a vegan is a political decision. Every year in the United States alone, more than 20 billion animals are slaughtered by the meat industry. Outrage over the inhumane treatment of livestock has pushed millions of people to make the switch to a meat-free lifestyle. For others, the switch is out of concern for their health. Meat-free diets have been proven to help prevent a number of serious diseases including type 2 diabetes, heart disease, and cancer. A vegan lifestyle may also help you achieve a healthy body weight; improved energy levels; and a longer, more fulfilling life. Other reasons for switching to a vegan diet include concern for the environment, religious reasons, or a combination of any or all of these.

If you are curious about the vegan lifestyle and the benefits it provides, then this is the right book for you. Here you will find in-depth reviews of common motivations for going vegan and information regarding the difference between vegans and vegetarians. You will also find evidence-supported explanations of the many health benefits, as well as 150 delicious vegan recipes that will help you start and maintain your new vegan lifestyle.

CHAPTER ONE

What Is the Vegan Diet?

Vegans are people who do not eat or use animal products. Englishman Donald Watson coined the term in 1944 when he sought to create a specific name for non-dairy vegetarians. That same year, Watson along with twenty-four others founded the Vegan Society, the oldest vegan society currently still operating. Its founding day is celebrated every year as World Vegan Day.

Though the original definition of veganism was meant to include vegetarians who did not consume eggs or dairy products, the definition changed and developed over time. In 1951, the Vegan Society expanded the definition, saying that, "veganism is the doctrine that man should live without exploiting animals" (Walter, et al.). Today, the Vegan Society defines veganism as "a way of living that seeks to exclude, as far as possible and practicable, all forms of exploitation of, and cruelty to, animals for food, clothing, and any other purpose."

THE PRINCIPLES OF VEGANISM

Dietary Veganism: Animals should not be exploited for food. Individuals should abstain from eating meat, seafood, poultry, eggs, milk, cheese, and other dairy products.

Environmental Veganism: Animal products should not be used because the harvesting and farming of animals is damaging to the environment and an unsustainable practice.

Ethical Veganism: All sentient beings have the right to live a life free from suffering and exploitation at the hands of human beings.

HOW ARE VEGANS AND VEGETARIANS DIFFERENT?

The simple answer is that vegans *are* vegetarians. Veganism developed out of vegetarianism and is founded on many of the same principles. Vegans follow all of the same dietary rules and restrictions in terms of not eating meat. They take things one step further, however, by eliminating all animal products from their diets—this includes meat, eggs, milk, cheese, and other dairy products. Some vegans also choose not to use clothing or other products that are derived from animal sources. These may include honey, fur, leather, silk, wool, whey, lard, and beeswax. Strict vegans may also refrain from using cosmetics and other products that have been tested on animals.

While vegetarianism has been practiced since ancient times in India and Greece, the term *vegetarian* didn't come into popular use until the nineteenth century. A number of people followed a meat-free diet during the eighteenth and nineteenth centuries, but it wasn't until 1847 that the British Vegetarian Society was founded. The foundation of this society resulted in an increase in the number of individuals practicing vegetarianism in the United Kingdom. Over the next fifty years, there was a great deal of correspondence between members of the Vegetarian Society regarding the consumption of eggs and dairy products. Certain individuals such as Henry Salt suggested that vegetarianism was more than just a matter of human health—it was a moral issue.

With the founding of the Vegan Society in 1944, the two movements began to grow in separate directions. Though both are founded on the same principles, vegans and vegetarians differ slightly on the issue of animal welfare versus animal rights. While vegetarians do not eat meat, they still consume certain animal products including eggs, milk, and cheese. Vegans, on the other hand, consider the use of animals for food a form of exploitation. In 1951, the vice-president of the Vegan Society, Leslie Cross, wrote that, "Veganism is not so much welfare as liberation, for the creatures and for the mind and heart of man; not so much an effort to make the present relationship bearable, as an uncompromising recognition that because it is in the main one of master and slave, it has to be abolished before something better and finer can be built."

WHY DO PEOPLE BECOME VEGAN?

For many individuals, veganism is more than just a dietary preference. According to Animal Equality, an international nonprofit based in London, veganism is "a lifestyle that does not cause suffering, harm, or death to animals ... allowing animals to be free to choose the way they want to live." Though not all people who follow a vegan diet do so for moral reasons, concern for animal rights and welfare is one of the most common reasons people become vegan.

Some of the other motivations for becoming vegan include: health reasons, religious affiliation, dietary preference, and environmental concern.

Animal Rights/Welfare

One of the most common reasons people become vegan is opposition to the treatment of animals in the industrial animal agriculture industry. The term *industrial agriculture* is often used to describe the methods through which livestock including cattle, poultry, and fish are raised for food. Also called factory farming, industrial agriculture is designed to produce high-quality livestock using both modern machinery and medical science. The Worldwatch Institute, an environmental research organization based in Washington, D.C., recently revealed that almost 75 percent of the word's poultry is produced through factory farming.

Proponents for this method of animal production suggest that it is highly efficient, reducing costs for companies and improving the quality of the end product. Opponents of factory farming argue that it is harmful to the environment and cruel to animals. Many vegans argue that it is abusive and unethical to kill animals to meet human needs. Animals that end up in the industrial agriculture system do not have a choice in how they live their lives and they often suffer violent deaths.

* * *

If you find that you are having a hard time giving up meat, pay a visit to a local farm or animal shelter to remind yourself why you made the switch to a vegan lifestyle. Spending some time with the animals might make it a little more difficult to imagine eating one.

* * *

Another issue connected to animal rights and veganism is animal testing. In many cases, cosmetics, medicines, and other products are tested on laboratory animals before being made available for use by humans. The pharmaceuticals industry runs on the principle of speciesism—that animals are somehow inferior to humans and thus do not deserve the same rights. Even products that are designed to protect animals (such as various flea/tick products) may have harmed or killed a significant number of animals during the testing phase. People who go vegan out of concern for animal rights often do so as a means of not supporting animal testing.

Health Reasons

For many individuals, going vegan is a choice made based on health reasons. A number of studies have been conducted that show the health benefits associated with a plant-based diet. For example, individuals who follow a vegan diet tend to exhibit lower cholesterol levels and have a decreased risk for developing certain cancers. Eliminating meat and animal products from the diet may also be used as a weight-loss measure. By eliminating animal products, one can significantly reduce one's daily calorie intake. See the following chapter for more on the health benefits of veganism.

Religious Affiliation

For some, the choice to become vegan is the result of religious beliefs or affiliation. Several of the world's most common religions advocate for healthy eating, and some even advocate for vegetarianism specifically. Some of the founding principles of Christianity, for example are love, mercy, and compassion—people who become vegan for religious reasons often suggest that this love, mercy, and compassion should be extended to animals as well as humans.

Judaism also provides support for a vegan diet. In the first chapter of Genesis, it is written that "God said, 'Behold, I have given you every plant yielding seed that is on the surface of all the earth, and every tree which has fruit yielding seed; it shall be food for you'" (Gen. 1:29).

Upon his creation, Adam was charged with the duty of naming and caring for the animals God created. It was not said that these animals were created as food for humans.

Both Hinduism and Buddhism, too, advocate for a plant-based diet. Ancient Hindus believed that humans should not kill in order to live—living a vegan lifestyle is a means of limiting cruelty or violence to other living things. One of the most important principles of Buddhism is to coexist peacefully with the world around us. Living a vegan lifestyle is the result of mercy and compassion for animals that is also tied in to the idea of karma. Karma is the belief that your actions in this life will affect your station in the next life. A common saying in Buddhist culture is that "good is rewarded with good; evil is rewarded with evil." Choosing a vegan lifestyle is choosing to do good in regard to the treatment of animals.

Dietary Preference

Some people simple do not like the taste or texture of meat and other animal products. In these cases, the choice to go vegan may not be a conscious choice—it may simply be a dietary preference.

Environmental Concern

People who go vegan as a result of environmental concern often cite the issue of sustainability. Rather than utilizing crops for human consumption, millions of tons of grain, corn, and soybeans are funneled through the industrial agriculture system. The Worldwatch Institute suggests that the meat industry is the primary reason why millions of people around the globe are starving when there is more than enough food available to feed the entire planet. The Worldwatch Institute states that "meat consumption is an inefficient use of grain—continued growth in meat output is dependent on feeding grain to animals, creating competition for grain between affluent meat-eaters and the world's poor."

Not only does the rearing of livestock require the inefficient use of crops, but it can also be damaging to the environment itself. Livestock production requires the use of valuable resources such as land, fossil fuels, and water—it may also contribute to air pollution, land degradation, deforestation, and decline in biodiversity. For some people, going vegan is an ethical response to the livestock industry's abuse and exploitation of the environment.

. . . .

Did you know that the United States produced over 26 billion pounds of beef in 2011 for a total revenue of over $45 billion? That equates to more than 34 million head of cattle—about 26 million steers and heifers along with 7 million dairy cows.

. . . .

As you can see, people become vegan for a variety of reasons. No one reason is superior to another, and many people become vegan for *all* of the reasons listed above. Ultimately, you need to decide where you stand on these issues and whether veganism might be a fitting lifestyle for you. Before you make a decision, take the time to learn as much as you can about veganism so you know exactly what you are getting into.

CHAPTER TWO

The Health Benefits of Going Vegan

Individuals who follow a vegan lifestyle are often misunderstood—they are seen as fanatical animal rights activists who spend their days munching on carrots and bean sprouts. What many people do not realize is that a vegan diet is significantly better for you than the traditional meat-based diet that has become so prolific in modern Western culture. Not only does the vegan diet provide your body with a variety of healthy nutrients, but it can also prevent or relieve some of the major diseases affecting the population. Individuals who follow a vegan lifestyle exhibit much lower instances of cardiovascular disease, type 2 diabetes, arthritis, osteoporosis, and several types of cancer. Going vegan is not just the right choice for those who want to show support for animal rights—it is also the right choice for those who are serious about taking care of their bodies.

OVERVIEW OF HEALTH BENEFITS ASSOCIATED WITH VEGANISM

The vegan lifestyle has been linked with a variety of significant health benefits from reduced risk for disease to improved nutrition. The following list provides a brief peek into the health benefits of going vegan:

Nutritional Benefits:

- Reduced intake of saturated fats—improved cardiovascular health
- High in fiber—improved digestive health, helps fight colon cancer
- Increased intake of magnesium—aids in the absorption of calcium, which is essential for bone health

- High in antioxidants—help repair and protect against cellular damage caused by free radicals (atoms or groups of atoms with unpaired electrons, which can cause damage in their search for matching electrons).
- Increased intake of potassium—helps reduce acidity in the body, stimulates the kidneys for healthy elimination of toxins
- High levels of vitamin C—boosts healing and gum health, supports a health immune system

Disease-Prevention Benefits

- Improves cardiovascular health by eliminating dairy and meat while eating whole grains and nuts
- Eliminating animal products will eliminate all dietary cholesterol
- Easier to follow than the diet recommended by the American Diabetic Association for type 2 diabetes
- May stop the progress or reverse the effects of certain cancers, including prostate cancer
- Reduces the chance of developing colon cancer and breast cancer
- Increased intake of fruits and vegetables helps prevent macular degeneration
- Reduced consumption of dairy products may provide relief from the symptoms of rheumatoid arthritis

Physical Benefits

- Eliminating unhealthy foods often results in weight loss and lowered BMI
- Contributes to higher energy levels and increased endurance during physical activity
- Vitamins in nuts and vegetables help improve skin clarity and complexion
- Eliminating dairy and meat will help reduce bad breath and body odor
- Contributes to improved hair and nail growth, strength, and appearance
- May provide relief for those who suffer from migraines

Did you know that you can get all the protein you need on a daily basis without eating a single bite of meat? Even professional athletes who operate at an extremely high physical level get all the protein they need to keep their bodies and their muscles strong by consuming only plant-based foods. In fact, a vegan diet keeps athletes at the top of their game all day long because it is free from the cholesterol, saturated fat, and artificial additives found in animal products, which can slow athletes down.

COMMON MALADIES ASSOCIATED WITH MEAT CONSUMPTION

There is a great deal of controversy regarding whether the benefits of meat consumption outweigh the risks. Many health professionals advocate for the consumption of red meat because it is a source of complete proteins, which are essential for healthy renewal and repair of the body. Red meat is also a good source of iron, zinc, and B vitamins. Proponents of plant-based diets, on the other hand, argue that red meat is often high in saturated fat, low in fiber, and often treated with growth hormones and other chemicals that could be harmful to human health.

In order to truly understand the health benefits of a vegan lifestyle, you must first understand the problems associated with a meat-based diet. The overconsumption of meat in Western cultures has been linked to increased risk for cancer, heart disease, type 2 diabetes, and a number of other serious health conditions. Below you will find an in-depth explanation of some of the most common maladies associated with the consumption of meat.

Cancer

According to the World Health Organization, dietary factors are to blame for at least 30 percent of all cancers seen in modern Western culture. When researchers first began to study the correlation between diet and disease, studies conducted in Europe showed that individuals who followed a vegetarian diet were almost 40 percent less likely to develop cancer than were individuals who regularly consumed meat (Barnard, et al.). In the United States, a similar study was performed using a group of Seventh-day Adventists.

Seventh-day Adventists generally abstain from alcohol and tobacco products and about half of the population follows a vegetarian diet. This allowed researchers to isolate the effects of meat consumption from other dietary and lifestyle factors. The results of this study, published in the *Journal of Clinical and Experimental Pharmacology and Physiology* in May 1982, also suggested that those who avoided meat had a reduced risk for cancer (Rouse, et al.).

In 2007, the American Institute for Cancer Research and the World Cancer Research Fund published a report titled *Food, Nutrition, Physical Activity, and the Prevention of Cancer: A Global Perspective.* This report provided a review of the dietary and lifestyle habits of a variety of cultures in correlation to each culture's cancer risk. Using the scientific and medical evidence that had been discovered to date, a panel of scientists judged certain factors on their potential to modify the risk of cancer. This panel judged that the evidence suggesting red meats and processed meats are a cause of colorectal cancer is convincing. Evidence was also suggestive that red meats, processed meats, and animal foods containing iron contribute to increased risk for cancer of the lungs, pancreas, stomach, prostate, esophagus, and endometrium (Marmot, et al.).

Heart Disease

It has long been suggested that the saturated fat and cholesterol content of red meat contribute to increased risk for heart disease; however, a recent article published in the journal *Nature Medicine* suggests that there may be an additional factor. L-carnitine is a compound found in abundance in red meat, and the consumption of this compound results in the production of another compound in the gut called trimethylamine-N-oxide (TMAO). Studies conducted using mice have shown that TMAO causes atherosclerosis, which often results in clogged arteries and contributes to an increased risk for heart attack (Murphy, et al.).

Type 2 Diabetes

Type 2 diabetes occurs when the body's insulin secretion becomes impaired. As a result, the body is unable to control blood glucose levels, which can lead to dangerous spikes and crashes in blood sugar. Frank Hu, a professor of epidemiology, states that there are three components in red meat that contribute to an increased risk for diabetes: sodium, nitrates, and iron. Sodium, found in table salt and processed meats, has been shown to increase blood pressure and may also cause insulin resistance. Insulin resistance occurs when the body fails to respond appropriately to the production of insulin. This often leads to the overproduction of insulin and a condition called *hyperglycemia*.

Like sodium, both nitrites and nitrates have been shown to induce a similar reaction. Additionally, they may also impair the ability of pancreatic beta cells to function normally. The third component, iron, is a mineral that is essential for the healthy function of the human body. In high levels, however, it can lead to oxidative stress, cell damage, and chronic inflammation. This is especially dangerous for individuals with hereditary hemochromatosis—a condition in which the digestive tract absorbs too much iron. Heme iron, the type of easily absorbed iron found in red meat, is instrumental in causing beta cell damage.

Obesity

According to a study conducted at the Johns Hopkins Bloomberg School of Public Health, overconsumption of meat may increase your risk for becoming obese (Wang and Beydoun). This information conflicts with the principles of high-protein diets such as the Atkins diet. Studies have shown, however, that such high-protein diets do not provide long-term results, and that Atkins Diet participants often experience reversed or stalled weight loss after as little as six months on the program. In contrast to meat-based diets, vegan diets are naturally low in fat, which helps reduce your caloric intake and manage your weight. Recent research suggests that meat eaters have an obesity rate of three times that of vegetarians and nine times that of vegans. In fact, on average, an adult following the vegan diet weighs ten to twenty pounds less than an adult following a meat-based diet.

Cognitive Decline

Throughout the course of your life, iron gradually accumulates in your cells and tissues. This build-up can eventually lead to free radical damage and mitochondrial decay. Dr. George Bartzokis, professor of psychology at UCLA, states that excess iron in the brain "contributes to the development of abnormal deposits of proteins associated with several prevalent neurodegenerative diseases, such as Alzheimer's disease, Parkinson's disease, and dementia" (Bartzokis, et al.). Even adults who do not suffer from any of these diseases may still exhibit decreased cognitive abilities in connection with higher brain iron levels.

In 2001, along with a number of his colleagues, Bartzokis published the results of a study regarding the connection between hysterectomy and increased iron levels in the brain (Bartzokis, et all). Though the results of the study are primarily focused on the link between premenopausal hysterectomy and the onset of neurodegenerative disease, they can also be used as support for the argument that the consumption of red meat is bad for your health.

According to the American Dietetic Association (ADA), the recommended daily intake of iron is no more than 18 milligrams for females aged 19 to 50 and 8 milligrams for males older than 19. A single 3-ounce serving of lean sirloin beef contains about 3 milligrams of iron. Many people, when they eat a steak, eat more than the recommended serving size—often two or three times more. Studies suggest that men tend to consume more red meat than women, and a single large steak could put you over your daily recommended intake of iron. The overconsumption of red meat throughout the course of an entire lifetime is likely to result in excess iron build-up in the brain, which increases your risk for developing neurodegenerative diseases like Alzheimer's disease and Parkinson's (Anderson LEF).

Bone Diseases

Studies have shown that overconsumption of red meat can have an adverse effect on the health of your bones. One reason is that meat products, when compared to vegetable foods, tend to contain more phosphorus than calcium. Unbalanced phosphorus/calcium ratios can lead to hyperparathyroidism, a condition that leads to hypocalcaemia, which, if left untreated, often leads to bone disease. The process of digesting red meat can also have a damaging effect on your body. The process through which meat-based proteins are digested leaves acidic residue in the body. These acids need to be neutralized with alkalizing minerals, and if your diet doesn't contain enough of these minerals, the acids may be leached from your bones.

PLANT-BASED VERSUS MEAT-BASED DIETS

The information provided in the previous section should give you an understanding of how and why the consumption of meat can be damaging to your health. In order to truly understand the vegan diet, however, you need to be able to correlate the negative effects of a meat-based diet with the benefits of a plant-based diet. In this section you will learn the extent to which meat consumption can increase your risk for serious disease while eating a diet based on plant foods can decrease your risk.

Cancer

There are a number of hypotheses regarding the connection between meat consumption and increased cancer risk. One hypothesis is that meat often contains certain carcinogenic compounds that may increase an individual's risk for developing cancer. Some of these compounds such as heterocyclic amines (HCA) and polycyclic aromatic hydrocarbons (PAH) are formed when meat is cooked or processed. Both of these compounds have been linked to increased cancer risk.

The high saturated fat content of meat may also increase your body's hormone production, which could also increase your risk for hormone-related cancers, namely breast cancer and prostate cancer. The Physicians Committee for Responsible Medicine published a report titled "Meat Consumption and Cancer Risk," which summarized the findings of numerous case-control and cohort studies regarding the connection between diet and cancer risk. In this report, it is noted that women who consume meat on a daily basis have risk of breast cancer almost nine times higher than women who rarely eat meat. This report also references a study involving over 148,000 adult participants whose dietary habits were followed since 1982. The individuals who had the highest intake of red and processed meats showed up to a 50-percent higher risk for colon cancer than did other groups (PCRM).

A study conducted in the UK and published in the journal *Cancer Epidemiology Biomarkers and Prevention* gauged the impact of a vegetarian diet on the risk for cancer. Compared to those who consumed meat on a regular basis, vegetarians showed a 10-percent reduced risk for cancer. The results of the study also showed a correlation between a vegetarian diet and reduced risk for stomach cancer, esophageal cancer, colon cancer, and pancreatic cancer. When the results between the different types of vegetarian diet were compared, those who followed a vegan diet were shown to have the most significant reduction in cancer risk (Tantamango-Bartley, et al.).

Dr. T. Colin Campbell, a nutritional researcher at Cornell University, states that "the vast majority of all cancers, cardiovascular diseases, and other forms of degenerative illness can be prevented simply by adopting a plant-based diet."

Heart Disease

The American Heart Association (AMA) identifies saturated fat and cholesterol as two of the primary factors contributing to increased risk for heart disease. Saturated fat is found in animal foods and dairy products. These foods also contain cholesterol. The AMA recommends a daily intake of saturated fat equal to less than 7 percent of your total daily calories, and cholesterol intake should be limited to 300 milligrams per day.

There are two types of dietary cholesterol: high-density lipoproteins (HDL) and low-density lipoproteins (LDL). It is important to maintain a healthy balance of both, with HDL, or good cholesterol, higher than LDL, bad cholesterol, at a ratio of less than 4:1. The average American male has a ratio around 5:1 while vegetarians average around 2.8:1.3. Every 1-percent reduction in cholesterol level results in a 2-percent reduction in your risk for heart disease.

Type 2 Diabetes

A recent study published in the *Journal of the American Medicine Association: Internal Medicine* provides new evidence to support the hypothesis that consumption of red meat increases the risk for type 2 diabetes (Pan, et al.). This study was conducted by researchers at the National University of Singapore using data collected from almost 150,000 individuals. The results of the study suggest that increased consumption of red meat correlates to a 48-percent increase in risk for diabetes, while reduced consumption correlates to a 14-percent decrease in risk for diabetes (Pan, et al.). The study also found that substituting whole grains and nuts for meat helped substantially lower the risk for diabetes.

Obesity

The study conducted at the Johns Hopkins Bloomberg School of Public Health regarding meat consumption and obesity yielded results to support the hypothesis that meat consumption is linked to body mass index (BMI) and central obesity. The data showed that individuals who consumed more meat on a regular basis were 33 percent more likely to have central obesity than those who ate less meat (Wang and Beydoun). Additionally, higher intakes of meat products were associated with higher BMI and waist-circumference, measurements. In contrast, participants who exhibited higher fruit and vegetable intake had lower BMI and waist-circumference, measurements (Wang and Beydoun).

Cognitive Decline

One of the most serious forms of cognitive decline is the neurodegenerative disease known as Alzheimer's. This disease is not a natural result of aging—it is caused by damage to and death of brain cells. Recent research suggests that there may be a correlation between the saturated fat and cholesterol found in animal products and the risk for neurodegenerative diseases like Alzheimer's and Parkinson's.

A study conducted by the Vanderbilt School of Medicine and published in the *American Journal of Medicine* in 2006 provides support for the hypothesis that vegetable-based diets help reduce cognitive decline. More than 1,800 participants in the study were followed for one year and evaluated based on their consumption of fruit and vegetable juices. Individuals who drank juices at least three times per week showed a hazard ratio for Alzheimer's disease of 0.24, while those who drank juice less than once a week had a ratio of 0.84 (Dai, et al.). The results of other studies indicate that the antioxidants found in a vegetarian diet can help to reduce or reverse the damaging effects of free radicals in the brain, slowing or preventing numerous forms of cognitive decline.

Bone Diseases

In 2001, the American Society for Clinical Nutrition conducted a study regarding the correlation between an increased ratio of dietary animal to vegetable protein and increased risk for bone loss and fracture (Sellmeyer, et al.). This study followed a group of 1,035 postmenopausal women, measuring their protein intake via questionnaire and their bone mineral density by X-ray. The results of the study showed that women who consumed a high ratio of animal to vegetable protein experienced more rapid bone loss in the neck as well as a risk for hip fracture almost four times higher than those who consumed animal protein at a lower ratio to vegetable protein (Sellmeyer, et al.).

Another study, published in the European *Journal of Nutrition* in 2001, studied the correlation between diet and bone mineral density (Tucker, et al.). It was hypothesized that a fruit- and vegetable-based diet would show a correlation to higher bone mineral density at the start of the study and reduced bone loss over the course of the study. The results of the study did indeed support the hypothesis: Individuals who consumed more plant-based proteins exhibited greater bone mineral density and experienced lower bone loss over the four years covered in the study (Tucker, et al.).

CHAPTER THREE

Making the Transition:
Changing Your Diet

In this chapter you will learn how to make gradual changes to your diet and how to assess yourself during the transition. You will also receive tips for making sure you receive adequate nutrition so you can enjoy as many benefits as possible in switching to the vegan diet.

GRADUALLY GOING VEGAN

After reading the benefits associated with a vegan diet and lifestyle, you may be excited to make the change. No matter how excited you are, you should take a step back and think about how you are going to make the process of going vegan a gradual one. If you make the switch too quickly, it could have negative effects on your body and it could make it more difficult for you to stick to the diet. Even though most people do not eat the same exact meals every day, if you suddenly make a drastic change to your diet, it could put stress on your digestive system, especially if you suddenly increase your intake of dietary fiber.

The key is to make small changes to your diet over a significant period of time. Your first step, rather than cutting out all animal products, should be to add more fruits, vegetables, grains, and legumes to your diet. You might also think about reducing the amount of meat you use in your recipes to balance out the extra vegetables. Next, try eliminating meat from one meal a day or several meals a week. After a few weeks of this, try incorporating some meatless substitutes in your favorite recipes: Try vegan crumbles in place of meat in your spaghetti sauce or tofu in your stir-fry.

Once you've successfully eliminated meat from your diet, you can move on to eggs, cheese, and other dairy products. For many people, cheese is the hardest thing to give up, so you may want to save that for last. Start out by replacing dairy milk with dairy-free alternatives such as soy milk, almond milk, and coconut milk. Start using egg replacer in your baking recipes and try to reduce the amount of cheese you use. When you are ready, swap out cheese for the many tasty vegan-friendly alternatives such as soy or rice cheese. If you make the transition to a vegan lifestyle slow and methodical, your body will have time to adjust to the changes, and you won't feel like you are suddenly depriving yourself of all the foods you have gotten used to consuming.

. . . .

Did you know that soy is very high in phytoestrogens, which can mimic estrogen in the human body? Too much estrogen can lead to a number of health problems, so try to limit the amount of soy-based foods you eat.

. . . .

ASSESSING YOURSELF DURING THE TRANSITION

As you make the transition, you may want to keep some kind of journal to track your progress. For many people, making the switch to a vegan diet is about losing weight or improving health—if this is the case with you, record your body weight and measurements before you start the transition and retake your measurements every two weeks or so. You may also want to take note of other physical changes you experience such as clearer skin, shinier hair, and stronger nails.

Many people who make the switch to a vegan diet notice dramatic improvements in their energy levels and overall well-being. Take note of your energy level throughout the day. Does it fluctuate throughout the day or has it started to level out, leaving you feeling refreshed and energized all day long? You may also experience some psychological changes. For example, you may find yourself feeling more positive. Or, you will no longer feel as if your mind is controlled by thoughts of food and that you are simply eating for the sake of eating *and* actually enjoying your meals.

Another surprising change you may notice is that food will begin to be more flavorful. You might think that making so many eliminations from your diet would have the opposite effect, but for many people, going vegan results in food becoming more enjoyable and more flavorful.

Every person's experience will be different, and to truly realize the benefits and changes you experience, keep a journal of your daily progress. Not only will this help you to see how far you have come, but it will also be a great tool to use in sharing your vegan lifestyle with others.

Avoid Common Mistakes

Making the switch to a vegan lifestyle can be a challenge and there are several common mistakes you will want to avoid if you can. One of the most common mistakes new vegans make is relying on prepared foods and snacks. Even though these foods may be vegan-friendly, they may also be full of empty calories that do not actually provide your body with nutrition. Living a healthy and balanced vegan lifestyle will require you to do some cooking for yourself at home so you get the full nutritional benefits of the foods you are eating.

Another mistake people make is not eating enough. It is important to remember that fruits and vegetables contain fewer calories (but more nutrients) than animal products, so you may need to eat higher quantities of food to feel full. On a related note, you should always carry with you some vegan-friendly snacks such as dried fruit or nuts so you have something to munch on when you get hungry. If you have healthy snacks on hand, you will be less likely to go for unhealthy options when you are desperate for something to eat.

Understanding Vegan Nutrition

After eliminating meat from your diet, you may be concerned about getting enough protein. The reality is that it can be difficult to achieve complete and healthy nutrition on a vegan diet unless you understand the basics. The American Dietetic Association states that proper nutrition can be achieved in following a vegan diet, but it does require some planning. The key to a healthy vegan diet is variety; eating a wide assortment of fruits, vegetables, leafy greens, nuts, whole grains, and legumes will help provide your body with all of the nutrients it needs.

The following chart identifies the daily requirements for some of the nutrients vegan diets are often found lacking.

DAILY NUTRITIONAL REQUIREMENTS			
NUTRIENT	CHILDREN	AVERAGE MALE	AVERAGE FEMALE
Protein	11 grams	56 grams	46 grams
Fat	30 grams	15–20% daily calories	15–20% daily calories
Calcium	800 milligrams	800 milligrams	800 milligrams
Vitamin D	10 micrograms*	10 micrograms	10 micrograms
Vitamin B12	1.0 micrograms	2 micrograms	2 micrograms
Iron	4.1 milligrams	6 milligrams	8.1 milligrams
Zinc	4 milligrams	9.4 milligrams	6.8 milligrams

* Based on the Dietary Reference Intakes: Estimated Average Requirements set forth by the National Academy of Sciences Institute of Medicine Food and Nutrition Board.

Protein

Many people mistakenly assume that eliminating meat from your diet means that it will be difficult to achieve your daily recommended intake of protein. In reality, a well-balanced vegan diet is full of plant-based protein. You do not need to worry about eating foods in certain combinations or plan your meals down to the very last detail to get your daily protein. All you have to do is eat a varied diet. Most foods contain some level of protein, but the best sources for vegetarian protein include:

- Almonds
- Broccoli
- Chickpeas
- Kale
- Lentils
- Peanut butter
- Peas
- Potatoes
- Rice
- Soy milk
- Spinach
- Tofu

. . . .

Make vegetable-based meals more filling by combining sources of protein and fiber. Try a noodle salad loaded with fiber from carrots and bell peppers topped with edamame for a boost of protein.

. . . .

Fat

After reading the last chapter, you may be wondering why fat is on the list of essential nutrients. While saturated fats are unhealthy in large quantities, your body does require some monounsaturated fat in order to be healthy. Some good sources of healthy fats include:

- Avocado
- Coconut
- Nut butters
- Nuts

- Olive oil
- Olives
- Seeds

Remember, fat should only account for 15 to 20 percent of your daily calorie intake, so use these foods sparingly.

Calcium

You probably grew up hearing that drinking milk is the key to building strong bones. In reality, milk may not be as high in calcium as you were led to believe. Calcium is, however, still an essential nutrient for maintaining bone health. This nutrient can be gleaned from a number of vegetarian sources including:

- Almond butter
- Bok choy
- Broccoli
- Dark green vegetables
- Fortified orange juice

- Fortified soy milk
- Soybeans
- Tempeh
- Tofu fortified with calcium sulfate

You may also want to consider taking a daily calcium supplement to make sure your daily need for calcium is met.

Vitamin D

Vitamin D is actually a hormone, and it plays a role in protecting bone health. The vegan diet does not naturally contain vitamin D, so you will need to be intentional about incorporating this nutrient into your diet. Some ways to get vitamin D include sun exposure, consumption of sun-exposed mushrooms, and dietary supplements. Many dietary supplements are not vegan friendly, so look for a supplement that has ergocalciferol as the main ingredient.

Vitamin B12

This vitamin is typically derived from animal sources and it is essential for maintaining healthy nerves and blood cells. Vitamin B12 is not actually produced by animals but by bacteria in the plants and soil in to which they are exposed. Some vegan sources of vitamin B12 include fortified nutritional yeast, tempeh, miso, and sea vegetables. The amount of the vitamin in these foods varies depending on the method of processing, so it is always a good idea to take a nutritional supplement or multivitamin.

Iron

Iron helps build strong muscles. This mineral is best absorbed by the body when eating in combination with vitamin C. Some good sources of vegetarian iron include leafy green vegetables, soybeans, lentils, dried beans, tahini, peas, watermelon, and kale. Not only are leafy greens such as kale, Swiss chard, and spinach good sources of iron, they also contain vitamin C, which helps your body to absorb the iron more efficiently.

Zinc

This mineral plays an important role in maintaining immune-system health and promoting healing of wounds. Zinc also supports healthy development in infants and children. Zinc can be found in a number of vegetarian sources, including whole grains, nuts, legumes, and fortified cereals.

. . . .

Did you know that humans are the only species that continues to drink milk beyond infancy? Humans are also the only species that consumes the milk of other species.

. . . .

CAUTIONS AND CAVEATS

After reading about the numerous benefits of switching to a vegan diet, you may still have a few questions. You may be wondering, for example, whether a vegan diet is safe for everyone. Certain diets are not recommended for children or for women who are pregnant or lactating. The easy answer to this question is, "Yes, the vegan diet is safe for children and pregnant women." The more complicated answer is, "Yes, but it requires a great deal of planning and fore-thought to achieve a healthy balance of nutrients."

Children and pregnant women have higher energy requirements and need a different balance of nutrients than the average adult. For this reason, it is unwise for children and pregnant women to engage in a vegan diet unless they have been cleared to do so by a physician and have nutritional guidance to ensure that their nutritional needs are met.

Before you switch a child to a vegan diet, consult your pediatrician to make sure the change won't have a negative effect. If your child is cleared for the vegan diet, make the transition slowly, using the steps outlined earlier in this chapter. Pregnant and lactating women should also consult their physicians before going on a vegan diet. It may not be a good idea to make the switch in the mid to late stages of pregnancy, especially if you are worried about getting all of the necessary nutrients. If you are determined to make the switch to a vegan diet, however, you can certainly do so as long as you do all the proper planning and preparation.

CHAPTER FOUR

Making the Transition:
Eating In and Dining Out

Making the switch to a vegan lifestyle is not something you can do at the drop of a hat. Not only does it take time to learn the basics, but it will also take time to eliminate all of the non-vegan food items from your kitchen and to stock up on vegan-friendly foods. In this chapter, you will learn exactly what you need to do in order to transform your kitchen into a vegan-friendly environment. You will also learn some valuable tips for transitioning into a healthy vegan diet.

KITCHEN CLEAN-OUT CHECKLIST

Before you start out, you may need to clean out your pantry. Many people choose to simply finish the animal products they have in stock before re-stocking with vegan-friendly food items. If you want to get started right away, another option is to give away the animal food products you have. Even though you have chosen to no longer consume these items, it is better to give the food away than to let it go to waste. Once you are ready to get going with your vegan diet, use this checklist to clean out your kitchen and pantry of non-vegan food items:

Bread and Grains

- ☐ Enriched breads
- ☐ Some bagels
- ☐ Some pancakes
- ☐ Some tortillas
- ☐ Some waffles

Beverages

- ☐ Soda/pop products
- ☐ Some beers
- ☐ Some grapefruit juices
- ☐ Some orange juices
- ☐ Some wines

Refrigerated Foods

- ☐ Bacon
- ☐ Cheese
- ☐ Cottage cheese
- ☐ Cream cheese
- ☐ Dairy milk
- ☐ Deli meat
- ☐ Sausages
- ☐ Sour cream
- ☐ Soy cheese
- ☐ Yogurt

Frozen Foods

- ☐ Frozen yogurt
- ☐ Ice cream
- ☐ Pizza
- ☐ Prepared entrées
- ☐ Sherbet

Snack Foods

- ☐ Barbecue-flavored chips
- ☐ Cereal bars
- ☐ Chocolate candy
- ☐ Gelatin snacks
- ☐ Gummy candies
- ☐ Marshmallows
- ☐ Red candies

Meat and Seafood

- ☐ Beef
- ☐ Canned fish
- ☐ Clams
- ☐ Fresh fish
- ☐ Mussels
- ☐ Other seafood
- ☐ Pork
- ☐ Poultry
- ☐ Scallops
- ☐ Shrimp (fresh and frozen)
- ☐ Smoked fish
- ☐ Wild game

Condiments

- ☐ Butter
- ☐ Fish sauce
- ☐ Honey
- ☐ Margarine
- ☐ Mayonnaise
- ☐ Oyster sauce
- ☐ Some barbeque sauces
- ☐ Some salad dressings
- ☐ Some steak sauces
- ☐ Worcestershire sauce

Canned/Dried Goods

- ☐ Beef broth
- ☐ Chicken broth
- ☐ Egg pasta
- ☐ Many canned soups
- ☐ Refined brown sugar*

- ☐ Refined white sugar*
- ☐ Refried beans
- ☐ Seafood broth
- ☐ Some jams/jellies

* Refined cane sugar is processed using bone char, which many vegans object to. However, no animal products are in the sugar itself. You can use unbleached cane sugar or other sugars labeled vegan if this is an issue for you.

See below for a list of the ingredients to look for when cleaning out your pantry and refrigerator.

GROCERY SHOPPING GUIDE

After making the switch to a vegan lifestyle, your first trip to the grocery store may be a little overwhelming. This grocery shopping guide will help you find the necessities for a healthy vegan diet while also providing you with plenty of meal options. Don't be tempted to think that just because you are eliminating meat and dairy from your diet that you are limiting your choices—there are countless delicious fruit and vegetables out there just waiting to be discovered. This grocery list will help get you started on your new vegan lifestyle:

Breads and Grains

- ☐ Brown-rice pastas
- ☐ Whole-grain breads
- ☐ Whole-grain pastas

- ☐ Whole grains (millet, quinoa, etc.)
- ☐ Whole-wheat couscous
- ☐ Wild or brown rice

Canned Goods

- ☐ Organic beans and vegetables
- ☐ Pasta sauces

- ☐ Vegetable broth

Dairy/Milk Replacements

- ☐ Egg replacer
- ☐ Non-dairy "cheese" products
- ☐ Rice, almond, soy, oat, or hemp milk

- ☐ Vegan butter-replacement spread

Refrigerated Food Items

- ☐ Hummus
- ☐ Meat substitutes
- ☐ Tempeh
- ☐ Tofu

Dessert Options

- ☐ Chocolate (bittersweet or 72 percent dark)
- ☐ Fresh-fruit sorbets
- ☐ Non-dairy ice treats
- ☐ Vegan chocolate mousse

Breakfast Items

- ☐ Organic steel-cut and instant oats
- ☐ Vegan cereals

Fruits and Vegetables

- ☐ All types of berries
- ☐ All types of melons
- ☐ All varieties of potatoes
- ☐ All varieties of mushrooms
- ☐ Apples
- ☐ Avocados
- ☐ Broccoli
- ☐ Brussels sprouts
- ☐ Dried fruit and fruit chips
- ☐ Fresh greens and lettuce
- ☐ Oranges and tangerines
- ☐ Seasonal produce

Frozen Food Items

- ☐ Vegan entrées
- ☐ Vegan meatless meatballs

Snack Options

- ☐ Brown rice cakes
- ☐ Fresh salsa or vegan dip
- ☐ Nut butters
- ☐ Popcorn (no butter)
- ☐ Raw or toasted nuts
- ☐ Trail mix
- ☐ Vegetable corn chips

. . . .

Did you know that many ethnic foods are vegetarian or vegan friendly? A variety of Indian, Asian, and Middle Eastern foods are made with primarily vegetable-based ingredients. Try some falafel with hummus, tofu pad thai, or vegetable curry.

. . . .

TIPS FOR READING FOOD LABELS

When you are first starting out on a vegan diet, it can be a little overwhelming. Not only do you have to eliminate a number of foods from your diet, but you also have to change your shopping strategy. You will no longer be able to simply pick things off the shelf—you will need to check the label on those food items to be sure they are free from animal products. Some food companies have begun to print the Vegan Society's trademark on their labels to let consumers know that the product has been certified vegan friendly.

If the label does not carry the Vegan Society trademark, that doesn't necessarily mean it is not vegan. Look for a claim that the product is suitable for vegetarians. If it is, the chances are good that it may also be vegan. In most cases, a quick read of the label and ingredients list will tell you whether or not the food contains animal products. Your first stop should be to check the allergy information—if the product contains milk or eggs, the product is not vegan. If milk and egg aren't listed in the allergy information, you should then check the ingredients list.

Food products containing the following ingredients are not vegan:

- Albumin
- Butter
- Butter acid
- Butter ester
- Butter fat
- Butter oil
- Casein
- Casein hydrolysate
- Caseinates
- Curds
- Custard
- Diacetyl
- Dried egg
- Egg solids
- Egg white
- Egg yolk
- Eggnog
- Gelatin (gel)

- Ghee
- Honey
- Lactalbumin
- Lactalbumin phosphate
- Lactoferrin
- Lactose
- Lactulose
- Lard
- Lysozyme
- Mayonnaise
- Meringue
- Meringue powder
- Milk protein hydrolysate
- Ovalbumin
- Potassium caseinate
- Powdered egg
- Pudding
- Recaldent

- Rennet casein
- Surimi
- Tallow

- Tagatose
- Whey
- Whey protein hydrolysate

If you're unsure of an ingredient, look it up online. There are several more comprehensive lists of hidden animal ingredients, including PETA's at http://www.peta.org/living/vegetarian-living/animal-ingredients-list.aspx.

The following ingredients may contain milk or eggs, but it is not always the case (read the allergen statement to be sure):

- ☐ Artificial butter flavor
- ☐ Bacterial cultures
- ☐ Caramel
- ☐ Chocolate
- ☐ Egg substitute
- ☐ Lactic acid starter culture
- ☐ Lecithin

- ☐ Macaroni
- ☐ Margarine
- ☐ Marzipan
- ☐ Marshmallows
- ☐ Nisin
- ☐ Nougat
- ☐ Pasta

EATING IN WITH FAMILY AND FRIENDS

When a friend or family member invites you over for a meal, the last thing you want to do is offend them by not eating the food they have prepared. It is always a good idea to let your host know ahead of time that you are a vegan. If your host is willing to accommodate you, explain to them the requirements of the diet. You can also offer to bring a vegan dish to share. This option saves your host from having to change the menu and also gives you an opportunity to share vegan food with others.

TIPS FOR DINING OUT

Though awareness of the vegan lifestyle is rapidly spreading, eating out can still be a challenge. If you know where to look, however, you can find a number of vegan-friendly restaurants, and you may even be surprised to find that some of your favorite restaurants have vegan options on the menu. Even if the restaurant doesn't specifically identify vegan dishes, you may be able to substitute or omit one or more ingredient.

Keep a list of vegan and vegetarian restaurants on hand for days when you can't handle cooking. You may be surprised how many restaurants have vegetarian options on the menu or can easily make accommodations for various dietary restrictions.

If you find yourself out with friends and family and don't have the option to look up a restaurant's menu before you visit, there are several vegan-friendly options you can almost always count on. At Chinese restaurants, stick to vegetable or tofu dishes—you can also go with vegetable fried rice as long as the eggs are omitted. Many Mexican dishes can be made vegan friendly by simply omitting the meat and cheese. (Try a bean burrito or make a meal out of refried beans and rice rolled up in fresh tortillas). When in doubt, you can always ask for a salad of chopped vegetables with a drizzle of olive oil and vinegar or a spritz of fresh lemon juice.

10 TIPS FOR A SUCCESSFUL TRANSITION

1. Start off slow. Don't try to rush the transition to a vegan lifestyle, because sudden increased consumption of dietary fiber could put stress on your digestive system. Try adding some extra vegetables to your favorite meals to replace some or all of the meat. You can also try vegan alternatives for cheese and milk.

2. Check the freezer section at your grocery store for meatless burgers, hot dogs, "chicken patties," and more. These products are a great option for a quick meal and they can be very helpful in making the transition to a meat-free lifestyle.

3. Dust off your apron and unpack your pots and pans. For people who are not used to cooking much for themselves, it can be tempting to live almost entirely off frozen vegan entrées. While these options are great for a quick meal, it is essential that you learn how to cook some basic meals for yourself, because whole foods are the most nutritious when they are fresh.

4. Do some research. Whatever your motives are for switching to a vegan lifestyle, read up on the issues that most interest you. Your friends and family are likely to have questions, so you should be prepared to answer them. Learning everything you can about the health benefits of a vegan lifestyle and animal rights will also help to keep you motivated.

5. Use the recipes in this book. The beauty of living a vegan lifestyle is that the options are endless when it comes to unique and flavorful combinations of ingredients, and your vegan culinary journey can begin with the recipes found here. Also, stock up on vegan and vegetarian cookbooks. Check out a few from the library to get yourself started or visit the PETA website for free recipes.

6. Familiarize yourself with Internet databases such as VegGuide.org and HappyCow.net to find vegetarian- and vegan-friendly restaurants in your area. You might want to make up a short list and keep it in your purse, wallet, or car so you have it when you need it.

7. Browse some vegan and vegetarian forums online. There are a number of forums and community chat rooms available that provide vegans with a means of sharing recipes, asking/answering questions, and simply providing support for one another. Some popular vegan forums include VeganForum.com, HappyCow.net, and VegTalk.org.

8. Try planning your meals as you get used to the vegan diet. It can be difficult at first to achieve the proper balance of macronutrients, vitamins, and minerals in a plant-based diet, but planning your meals ahead of time will help you to get all of the nutrients your body needs on a daily basis.

9. Take the opportunity to try new things. Many cultures follow vegan or near-vegan diets, so go out and try some ethnic food. Try some Indian vegetable curries, Mediterranean hummus and falafel, and Japanese vegetarian sushi.

10. Team up with a friend, join an online program, or find a vegan group in your community for support and help with the transition. If you have a spouse or partner who is willing to make the switch with you, the two of you will be able to help each other through the transition.

CHAPTER FIVE

Equipping Your Kitchen for the Vegan Diet

In preparing to make the switch to a vegan diet, you may want to consider making a few additions to your kitchen arsenal. Small appliances including a juicer, blender, dehydrator, and food processor will be incredibly useful in preparing vegan recipes. In addition to equipping your kitchen with handy appliances, you should also equip yourself with knowledge of vegan substitutes. It will take some time for you to get used to the vegan diet, and having knowledge of vegan friendly substitutes for meat, eggs, and dairy products will enable you to continue enjoying your favorite recipes.

USEFUL KITCHEN APPLIANCES

The following appliances are by no means a requirement, but having them on hand will increase the number of recipes you are able to prepare, or at least make preparing many of the recipes less time consuming.

Juicers

A juicer is an appliance used to separate the juice in fruits and vegetables from the pulp. Juicing has become extremely popular in the health and fitness world as a means of detoxification and weight loss. It is also an excellent addition to a healthy vegan diet. One of the main benefits of juicing is that it makes the nutrients in fresh fruits and vegetables easier for your body to absorb. It is also much easier to drink an eight-ounce glass of juice containing three or more servings of vegetables than it is to eat a large plate piled with veggies. Having a juicer in your kitchen will allow you to expand your recipe repertoire, enabling you to try new foods and to experiment with different flavors.

There are three different types of juicers: centrifugal juicers, masticating juicers, and triturating juicers. A centrifugal juicer is both easy to operate and clean, making it one of the most popular types of juicer available. These juicers work by grinding the produce through a grated basket, separating the pulp from the juice. Masticating juicers are motor driven and they work by kneading and grinding the raw material to extract the juice. These juicers work a little more slowly than other models, but they also operate at a lower heat to preserve the enzymes in the raw material. A triturating juicer utilizes a two-step process: The raw material is first crushed, and then it is pressed to extract the juice.

Blenders

A blender, commonly referred to as a liquidizer in the United Kingdom, is an electrical appliance used to puree or emulsify foods. Having a high-quality blender in your kitchen will enable you to make your own fruit and vegetable smoothies. The main benefit of smoothies over juices is that they retain their original dietary fiber content. The process of juicing removes the pulp and thus the fiber content from the raw materials. Blending the materials, on the other hand, preserves the fiber content. Healthy smoothies can be made using a variety of fruits and vegetables in whatever flavor combinations you like.

Dehydrators

A food dehydrator is an appliance that uses heat and airflow to remove moisture from food. Most fruits and vegetables consist of 80 to 95 percent water, and removing it helps prevent bacteria growth and also helps prevent the food from spoiling. A food dehydrator can be used to make own dried fruit slices to use in homemade trail mixes and other snacks or desserts. Food dehydrators come in a variety of styles. Most utilize stackable trays and incorporate either a solar or electric power source to provide heat.

Food Processors

A food processor is an appliance that can be used to peel, chop, or puree foods. It is similar in function to a blender, but it features interchangeable blades and disks. Another benefit of food processors over blenders is that they do not require the addition of liquid like blenders do. A food processor is a valuable tool in the vegan kitchen because it can be used to chop vegetables for salads and salsas, to grind nuts, to shred vegetables, and to knead dough. These appliances come in a variety of sizes ranging from mini 1½-cup processors to commercial grade 14-cup processors.

. . . .

Using a slow cooker is a great way to achieve moist, tender meals that are steeped in flavor. Combine some of your favorite vegetables with a flavorful pasta sauce and cook on low heat for several hours.

. . . .

MEAT SUBSTITUTES

No matter how dedicated to the vegan lifestyle you are, sometimes you might simply get the urge to sink your teeth into something hearty and substantial. Luckily, there are a number of vegan-friendly meat alternatives that you can incorporate into your favorite dishes, such as lasagna, stir-fries, and more.

Some popular meat alternatives include:

Seitan

A great source of vegetarian protein, seitan is made from wheat gluten. One 4-ounce portion contains 20 to 30 grams of protein.

Beans

Beans are favored by many vegans and vegetarians for their high protein content and versatility. Lentils, chickpeas, black beans, kidney beans, cannellini beans, and soybeans are just a few of the many you have to choose from. The protein content of beans varies from 12 to 29 grams per cup, cooked.

Tofu

Also known as bean curd, tofu is a soy product made by coagulating soy milk and pressing the curd into blocks. There are two different kinds of tofu: fresh and processed. Fresh tofu is typically sold in tubs, immersed in water—it may be soft/silken, firm, or extra firm. Processed tofu may be fermented, flavored, fried, dried, or frozen.

Tempeh

Tempeh is made from fermented soybeans and rice. It has a nutty flavor and is a good source of both protein and dietary fiber. What makes tempeh different from tofu is that it is made using the whole soybean, which gives it a firm, meat-like texture.

Broccoli

Although it may not be as high in protein as beans or other meat alternatives, broccoli still contains about 5 grams of protein per cup. Broccoli is also a great way to make your meals heartier so they fill you up.

Meatless Products

You have probably heard of burgers made from soy or veggies rather than meat. There are a number of other products made for vegans and vegetarians to be used as meat replacements, including mock turkey for holidays, fake bacon, breakfast "sausages," and more. Remember to read the ingredient lists carefully, and if it doesn't say "vegan" on the box, then it probably isn't.

. . . .

Remember that vegetarian meat substitutes won't taste exactly like the real thing. Learn to enjoy vegetarian and vegan foods for their own unique flavors and textures instead of endlessly comparing them to the foods you used to eat.

. . . .

EGG SUBSTITUTES

There are a number of simple substitutions you can make in your vegan cooking at home. For one egg, substitute one of the following:

- 2 tablespoons cornstarch (plus 3 tablespoons water)
- 2 tablespoons arrowroot powder
- Desired replacement for 1 egg (plus water)
- 1 tablespoon ground flaxseed (plus 3 tablespoons water, blended)
- 1 tablespoon whole flaxseeds (plus 4 tablespoons water, blended)
- 1 small banana, mashed (plus ¼ teaspoon baking powder, mixed)

- ¼ cup soft tofu (blended with liquid ingredients)
- ¼ cup unsweetened applesauce

DAIRY REPLACEMENTS

You can find a number of vegan-friendly substitutes for dairy products at your regular grocery store. If you live near a health-food store, you may be able to find even more options. Some popular vegan-friendly substitutes for dairy products include:

- **Milk**: soy milk, rice milk, almond milk, potato milk, water
- **Buttermilk**: soured soy or rice milk (add 1 tablespoon vinegar per cup of milk)
- **Cheese**: some rice cheeses, nut cheeses, and other cheeses
- **Cottage cheese or ricotta**: crumbled tofu

PART TWO

The Recipes

Meal Plans and Vegan Dishes for Any Occasion

. . . .

CHAPTER SIX

2-Week Vegan Meal Plan

In this chapter, you will find fourteen days' worth of meal plans. These are constructed using the recipes you will find in the following chapters. Feel free to mix and match the recipes to suit your preferences and supplement your meals with the quick and easy snacks as suggested.

DAY 1 MEAL PLAN

Breakfast
Maple Cinnamon Oatmeal
Lunch
Curried Lentil Soup
Dinner
Vegetable Lo Mein
Dessert/Snacks
Chocolate Peanut Butter Rice Bars
Hummus with veggie sticks

DAY 2 MEAL PLAN

Breakfast
Cinnamon Banana Pancakes
Lunch
Chopped Avocado Salad
Dinner
Quick and Easy Veggie Wrap
Dessert/Snacks
Tropical Fruit Smoothie with Chia Seeds
Apple with peanut butter

DAY 3 MEAL PLAN

Breakfast
Blueberry Muffins
Lunch
Creamy Cauliflower Soup
Dinner
Couscous-Stuffed Baked Tomatoes
Dessert/Snacks
Sweet Cinnamon Applesauce
1 to 2 slices vegan cheese

DAY 4 MEAL PLAN

Breakfast
Kiwi Raspberry Kale Smoothie
Lunch
Strawberry Walnut Salad
Dinner
Vegetarian Chili
Dessert/Snacks
Pomegranate Peach Smoothie
1 brown rice cake with almond butter

DAY 5 MEAL PLAN

Breakfast
Tropical Fruit Salad
Lunch
Sweet Potato Carrot Stew
Dinner
Stuffed Shells
Dessert/Snacks
Raw Coconut Fudge
Dry roasted peanuts

DAY 6 MEAL PLAN

Breakfast
Cinnamon Apple Raisin Oatmeal
Lunch
Red Cabbage Strawberry Salad
Dinner
Carrot Leek Risotto
Dessert/Snacks
Whipped Chocolate Mousse
Mixed fruit cup

DAY 7 MEAL PLAN

Breakfast
Refreshing Cucumber Celery Juice
Lunch
Creamy Cold Avocado Soup
Dinner
Crispy Corn Fritters
Dessert/Snacks
Cinnamon Baked Bananas
Vegan Vegetable Chips

DAY 8 MEAL PLAN

Breakfast
Whole Wheat Waffles
Lunch
Balsamic Sun-Dried Tomato Salad
Dinner
Penne with Mushrooms and Artichokes
Dessert/Snacks
Strawberry Green Tea Smoothie
Yellow corn chips with salsa

DAY 9 MEAL PLAN

Breakfast
Mixed Berry Mint Salad
Lunch
Asian Vegetable Soup
Dinner
Garlic Red Pepper Pasta
Dessert/Snacks
Maple-Glazed Poached Pears
Handful of vegan crackers

DAY 10 MEAL PLAN

Breakfast
Blueberry Banana Overnight Oats
Lunch
Tomato Cucumber Summer Salad
Dinner
Vegetable Fried Rice
Dessert/Snacks
Raspberry Lime Sorbet
Fresh orange slices

DAY 11 MEAL PLAN

Breakfast
Pumpkin Spice Muffins
Lunch
Roasted Tomato Basil Soup
Dinner
Fried Zucchini Fritters
Dessert/Snacks
Spiced Pumpkin Bars
Air-popped popcorn

DAY 12 MEAL PLAN

Breakfast
Steel-Cut Oatmeal with Dried Fruit
Lunch
Broccoli Almond Salad
Dinner
Rosemary Roasted Vegetables
Dessert/Snacks
Blueberry Sorbet
Apple cinnamon rice cakes

DAY 13 MEAL PLAN

Breakfast
Blueberry Mint Smoothie
Lunch
Chickpea Butternut Squash Stew
Dinner
Ratatouille
Dessert/Snacks
Cool Cranberry Coconut Smoothie
Pita chips with hummus

DAY 14 MEAL PLAN

Breakfast
Raw Buckwheat Porridge
Lunch
Cucumber Apple Pecan Salad
Dinner
Spinach Mushroom Lasagna
Dessert/Snacks
Fresh-Fruit Freeze Pops
Vegan crackers with vegan cheese slices

Check your local library for vegan or vegetarian cookbooks. Try out as many recipes you can to learn how to make vegetarian substitutions and to experience new flavors. If you find a book you really like, consider buying it for your kitchen.

CHAPTER SEVEN

Smoothies and Juices

Smoothies and juices are a quick and easy way to increase your daily intake of fresh fruits and vegetables. Juices can be incredibly simple to prepare with the help of a home juicer, and they are also a great way to combine unique flavors. Smoothies are ideal when you are looking for a beverage that has a little more substance, because they preserve the original fiber content of the produce. In this chapter you will find a variety of smoothies and juices incorporating fresh, natural flavors like kiwi, blueberry, banana, mint, lime, and more.

RECIPES INCLUDED IN THIS SECTION:

Blueberry Mint Smoothie

Mint is not only valued for its refreshing flavor, but it also helps to soothe inflammation and indigestion. This blueberry mint smoothie is so delicious, you may start treating it like a dessert.

½ CUP FRESH MINT LEAVES
1 CUP APPLE JUICE
3 CUPS FROZEN BLUEBERRIES
1 MEDIUM APPLE, CORED AND CHOPPED

1. In a blender, combine the mint and apple juice and blend until smooth and combined.

2. Add the remaining ingredients and pulse to chop, and then blend smooth.

3. Pour the smoothie into glasses and serve immediately.

Strawberry Green Tea Smoothie

Strawberries are an excellent source of vitamin C, which helps to promote the healing of wounds as well as gum and teeth health. Combined with green tea, this smoothie is full of health benefits.

1 CUP BREWED AND COOLED GREEN TEA
½ CUP FRESH MINT LEAVES
2 CUPS FROZEN STRAWBERRY HALVES
3 OR 4 ICE CUBES

1. Place the green tea and mint leaves in a blender and blend until liquefied.

2. Add the remaining ingredients and pulse to chop the berries and ice cubes.

3. Blend the mixture until smooth.

4. Pour into glasses and serve immediately.

Pomegranate Peach Smoothie

Pomegranate is a good source of vitamin C, beta-carotene, and antioxidants. It is known for its cleansing and detox properties and for reducing the risk for cancer.

1 CUP POMEGRANATE JUICE
1 CUP CHOPPED KALE LEAVES
2 FRESH PEACHES, PITTED AND SLICED
5 OR 6 ICE CUBES

1. Combine the pomegranate juice and kale in a blender and blend until smooth.

2. Add the remaining ingredients and blend until well combined.

3. Add more ice cubes, if needed, to thicken.

4. Pour the smoothie into glasses and serve immediately.

Cool Cranberry Coconut Smoothie

SERVES 2

Cranberries are incredibly rich in antioxidants, which help to repair cellular damage caused by free radicals. These berries also contain vitamin C and dietary fiber.

2 CUPS FROZEN CRANBERRIES
1 MEDIUM APPLE, CORED AND CHOPPED
1 CUP UNSWEETENED COCONUT MILK
½ CUP ORANGE JUICE
2 TABLESPOONS SHREDDED COCONUT

1. Combine the cranberries, apple, coconut milk, and orange juice in a blender and blend until smooth.

2. Pour the smoothie into 2 glasses and top with 1 tablespoon of shredded coconut each to serve.

. . . .

Because they're used for so many purposes beyond simple nutrition, coconuts are known as functional foods. For centuries, peoples of coastal Asia, the Pacific Islands, Mexico, South America, and Africa have used coconut oil for everything from spiritual ceremonies and maintaining healthy skin to treating a multitude of illnesses.

. . . .

Mango Melon Smoothie

SERVES 2

Mangoes are rich in both vitamin A and vitamin C. These two vitamins combined make mangoes an excellent immune-boosting fruit.

1 CUP CHOPPED WATERMELON
1 CUP CHOPPED HONEYDEW OR CANTALOUPE
1 CUP ORANGE MANGO JUICE
1 RIPE MANGO, PEELED, PITTED, AND CHOPPED
5 OR 6 ICE CUBES

1. Combine the watermelon, honeydew, and juice in a blender and blend until well combined.

2. Add the remaining ingredients and blend smooth.

3. Add more ice cubes, if desired, to thicken.

4. Pour the smoothie into glasses and serve immediately.

Tropical Fruit Smoothie with Chia Seeds

SERVES 2

This tropical fruit smoothie is cool and refreshing and full of tropical fruit flavor. Chia seeds are rich in omega-3 fatty acids, fiber, and antioxidants.

2 RIPE KIWIFRUIT, PEELED AND SLICED
1 CUP PINEAPPLE JUICE
2 TABLESPOONS CHIA SEEDS
1 CUP CHOPPED PINEAPPLE
1 BANANA, SLICED AND FROZEN
4 OR 5 ICE CUBES (OPTIONAL)

1. Combine the kiwi, pineapple juice, and chia seeds in a blender and blend smooth.

2. Add the remaining ingredients and blend until well combined.

3. Add ice cubes, if desired, to thicken.

4. Pour the smoothie into glasses and serve immediately.

Ginger Banana Smoothie

Bananas are an excellent source of vitamin B, which helps regulate mood and promote healthy sleep patterns. Ginger is known primarily for its detoxification benefits; it may also help to promote healthy digestion.

2 BANANAS, SLICED AND FROZEN
1 MEDIUM APPLE, CORED AND CHOPPED
½ CUP UNSWEETENED COCONUT MILK
1 INCH FRESH GINGERROOT, PEELED AND SLICED
5 TO 6 ICE CUBES (OPTIONAL)

1. Combine all of the ingredients in a blender and blend until smooth and well combined.

2. Add ice cubes and blend, if desired, to thicken.

3. Pour the smoothie into glasses and serve immediately.

Kiwi Raspberry Kale Smoothie

SERVES 2

Kiwi is rich in vitamin C, which not only helps to keep your gums and teeth healthy, but also promotes the healing of wounds. Combined with raspberry and kale, the kiwi in this recipe makes for a healthy and flavorful smoothie.

1 CUP CHOPPED KALE LEAVES
1 CUP ORANGE JUICE
1½ CUPS FROZEN RASPBERRIES
2 KIWIS, PEELED AND HALVED
4 OR 5 ICE CUBES

1. Combine the kale and orange juice in a blender and blend until liquefied.

2. Add the remaining ingredients and pulse to chop the frozen berries and ice cubes.

3. Blend the mixture until smooth.

4. Pour into two glasses and serve immediately.

Cilantro Cucumber Summer Smoothie

SERVES 2

Fresh cilantro is known for its refreshing scent and flavor, but it is also incredibly rich in antioxidants. This smoothie will help keep you cool in the summer while also providing heart-healthy benefits.

1 CUP CHOPPED ROMAINE LETTUCE
¼ CUP FRESH CILANTRO LEAVES
½ CUP ORANGE JUICE
3 TABLESPOONS FRESH LEMON JUICE
1 TABLESPOON FRESH LIME JUICE
1 SEEDLESS CUCUMBER, CHOPPED
1 MEDIUM APPLE, CORED AND CHOPPED
5 OR 6 ICE CUBES

1. In a blender, combine the lettuce, cilantro, orange juice, lemon juice, and lime juice and blend until smooth and combined.

2. Add the remaining ingredients and blend smooth.

3. Use more ice cubes, if desired, to thicken.

4. Pour the smoothie into glasses and serve immediately.

Broccoli Basil Green Smoothie

SERVES 2

Broccoli is a cruciferous vegetable with high dietary fiber content. Combined with the antibacterial and anti-inflammatory properties of basil, this smoothie is packed with powerful nutrients.

1 CUP FRESH BASIL LEAVES
1 CUP ORANGE JUICE
2 CUPS BROCCOLI FLORETS
5 OR 6 ICE CUBES

1. Place the basil leaves and orange juice in a blender.

2. Blend the mixture until smooth and then add the remaining ingredients.

3. Pulse to chop the broccoli and ice and then blend smooth.

4. Pour into glasses and serve immediately.

Watermelon Wake-Up Juice

Watermelon has a high water content, which makes it perfect for a yummy morning beverage. Not only is it highly refreshing, but watermelon also has antioxidant and anti-cancer properties.

1 SMALL SEEDLESS WATERMELON, CUBED
½ LIME, PEELED
1½ CUPS WATER

1. Place a container under the juicer's spout.

2. Feed the watermelon and lime through the juicer.

3. Stir the water into the juice and divide among glasses to serve.

Refreshing Cucumber Celery Juice

SERVES 1

Cucumbers are rich in potassium and phytosterols, two nutrients that help lower blood cholesterol levels. Celery contains silicon, which helps support bone and joint health.

3 LARGE STALKS CELERY, HALVED
1 CUCUMBER, QUARTERED
1 LARGE CARROT, HALVED
¼ BUNCH FRESH CILANTRO

1. Place a container under the juice's spout.

2. Feed the ingredients through the juicer, one at a time, in the order listed.

3. Stir the juice well.

4. Pour into a glass and serve immediately.

. . . .

If you have a high-powered blender, you can blend your juices in order to retain the fiber. The drinks will be smooth, nutritious, and delicious. Depending on your dietary needs and wants, you may decide to purchase this type of blender instead of a juicer.

. . . .

Berry Ginger Beet Juice

Beets are rich in iron, choline, and iodine. Studies have also shown that beets help oxygenate your blood, which, in turn, helps improve exercise performance and recovery.

1 CUP FRESH HALVED STRAWBERRIES

1 CUP WATER

1 MEDIUM-SIZED BEET, CHOPPED

1 MEDIUM APPLE, CORED AND CHOPPED

2 TABLESPOONS FRESH GRATED GINGERROOT

1. Combine the strawberries and water in a blender and blend smooth.

2. Add the remaining ingredients and blend until well combined.

3. Add more water, if needed, to thin.

4. Pour the juice into glasses to serve.

Sweet Spinach and Lime Juice

SERVES 2

Spinach is high in choline, a B-complex vitamin that helps to support healthy cognitive function. It is also a good source of iron, which supports healthy blood cells.

2 BUNCHES FRESH SPINACH LEAVES
1 MEDIUM APPLE, HALVED
1 SMALL LIME, HALVED

1. Peel, cut, deseed, and/or chop the ingredients as needed.

2. Place a container under the juicer's spout.

3. Feed the ingredients through the juicer, one at a time, in the order listed.

4. Stir the juice well.

5. Pour into glasses, and serve immediately.

Raspberry Radish Red Juice

Radishes are high in a variety of vitamins and minerals, including vitamin C, folic acid, and calcium. In fact, the leaves of the radish plant also contain a great deal of vegetarian protein.

6 SMALL RADISHES, WITH GREENS
1 CUP PACKED BABY SPINACH LEAVES
1 CUP FRESH RASPBERRIES
1 MEDIUM APPLE, HALVED
½ INCH FRESH GINGERROOT

1. Peel, cut, deseed, and/or chop the ingredients as needed.

2. Place a container under the juicer's spout.

3. Feed the ingredients through the juicer, one at a time, in the order listed.

4. Stir the juice well.

5. Pour into glasses and serve immediately.

Fresh Mint Mojito Juice

SERVES 2

This non-alcoholic juice is cool and refreshing—the ideal way to cool off in the summer or to wake yourself up in the morning.

1 CUCUMBER, QUARTERED
½ CUP PACKED FRESH MINT
¼ CUP PACKED FRESH BASIL LEAVES
1 LARGE APPLE, HALVED
3 TABLESPOONS FRESH LIME JUICE

1. Peel, cut, deseed, and/or chop the ingredients as needed.

2. Place a container under the juicer's spout.

3. Feed the ingredients through the juicer, one at a time, in the order listed.

4. Stir in the lime juice, pour into glasses, and serve immediately.

Fresh Fennel Juice Blend

Fennel is an herb that helps relieve anemia, indigestion, diarrhea, and respiratory problems. It has also been known to freshen breath.

2 MEDIUM-SIZED FENNEL BULBS
1 LARGE STALK CELERY
1 MEDIUM APPLE, HALVED
¼ BUNCH FRESH CILANTRO

1. Peel, cut, deseed, and/or chop the ingredients as needed.

2. Place a container under the juicer's spout.

3. Feed the ingredients through the juicer, one at a time, in the order listed.

4. Stir the juice well.

5. Pour into glasses and serve immediately.

Mixed Garden Greens Juice

This green juice recipe can easily be modified to utilize whatever greens and vegetables you have on hand. It is the perfect opportunity to make use of vegetables in your fridge that are about to spoil.

1 CUP FRESH BABY SPINACH
1 CUP FRESH ROMAINE LETTUCE
1 CUP FRESH KALE LEAVES
1 LARGE STALK CELERY
1 LARGE CARROT
½ BUNCH FRESH PARSLEY

1. Peel, cut, deseed, and/or chop the ingredients as needed.

2. Place a container under the juicer's spout.

3. Feed the ingredients through the juicer, one at a time, in the order listed.

4. Stir the juice well.

5. Pour into glasses and serve immediately.

. . . .

Take advantage of farmers' markets and consider joining a farm share program. Both options are a great way to get fresh, organic produce to fill out your new diet.

. . . .

Green Goddess Juice

Both spinach and kale are very nutrient-dense vegetables. This juice recipe is rich in a number of vitamins and minerals, including vitamin K, vitamin C, calcium, and iron.

1 CUP BABY SPINACH
1 CUP CHOPPED KALE LEAVES
1 SMALL SEEDLESS CUCUMBER, QUARTERED
1 CARROT
½ BUNCH FRESH MINT

1. Peel, cut, deseed, and/or chop the ingredients as needed.

2. Place a container under the juicer's spout.

3. Feed the ingredients through the juicer, one at a time, in the order listed.

4. Stir the juice well.

5. Pour into a glass and serve immediately.

Protein Power Punch

Both broccoli and flaxseed are good sources of vegetarian protein. This protein power punch also provides the cancer-fighting benefits of kale and collard greens.

1 BUNCH FRESH CURLY KALE
½ BUNCH COLLARD GREENS
1 SMALL HEAD BROCCOLI
1 LARGE CARROT
1 TABLESPOON FLAXSEED MEAL

1. Peel, cut, deseed, and/or chop the ingredients as needed.

2. Place a container under the juicer's spout.

3. Feed the first four ingredients through the juicer, one at a time, in the order listed.

4. Stir the flaxseed into the juice.

5. Pour into glasses and serve immediately.

CHAPTER EIGHT

Breakfast

Going vegan doesn't have to mean giving up all your favorites. Sure, eggs and bacons are a thing of the past; however, there are tons of great breakfast comfort foods that, with a little tweaking, can remain on your menu without guilt, problems, or loss of flavor. For more perfect day-starters, check out the juices and smoothies in Chapter 12.

RECIPES INCLUDED IN THIS SECTION:

Maple Cinnamon Oatmeal

Cinnamon Apple Raisin Oatmeal

Steel-Cut Oatmeal with Dried Fruit

Blueberry Banana Overnight Oats

Raw Buckwheat Porridge

Cinnamon Banana Pancakes

Peanut Butter Pancakes

Whole Wheat Waffles

Blueberry Muffins

Pumpkin Spice Muffins

Maple Cinnamon Oatmeal

SERVES 4

Oatmeal is a classic breakfast favorite. Add a little maple syrup and cinnamon for a hot breakfast that will keep you feeling satisfied all morning long.

1 CUP ROLLED OATS
2 CUPS WATER
1 TEASPOON VANILLA EXTRACT
1 CUP UNSWEETENED APPLESAUCE
1 TABLESPOON PURE MAPLE SYRUP
1 TEASPOON GROUND CINNAMON

1. Place the rolled oats in a blender or food processor and pulse until the oats are finely ground.

2. In a small saucepan, combine the water and vanilla extract over medium-high heat and then whisk in the ground oats.

3. Bring the mixture to a boil and then reduce the heat and simmer it for about 3 minutes.

4. Stir in the applesauce, maple syrup, and ground cinnamon.

5. Simmer the mixture for about 1 minute longer and then remove from heat.

6. Let sit for 2 or 3 minutes before serving hot.

Cinnamon Apple Raisin Oatmeal

SERVES 5 TO 6

This recipe is so sweet and delicious that you will have a hard time making your taste buds believe it is breakfast and not dessert.

1 CUP ROLLED OATS

2 CUPS WATER

1 TEASPOON VANILLA EXTRACT

1 CUP UNSWEETENED APPLESAUCE

1 MEDIUM APPLE, CORED AND CHOPPED

1 TABLESPOON PURE MAPLE SYRUP

1 TEASPOON GROUND CINNAMON

¼ CUP RAISINS

1. Place the rolled oats in a blender or food processor and pulse until the oats are finely ground.

2. In a small saucepan, combine the water and vanilla extract over medium-high heat and then whisk in the ground oats.

3. Bring the mixture to a boil and then reduce the heat and simmer it for about 3 minutes.

Stir in the applesauce, apple pieces, maple syrup, and cinnamon.

Simmer the mixture for about 1 minute longer and then remove from heat.

Let sit for 2 to 3 minutes and then serve hot, garnished with the raisins.

Steel-Cut Oatmeal with Dried Fruit

SERVES 4

This recipe is another one that you can make ahead of time. It is perfect for a lazy weekend or a quick breakfast if you have to get up early in the morning. Don't be afraid to swap in your favorite dried fruit or nuts for those suggested in the recipe.

2 CUPS UNSWEETENED ALMOND MILK

2 CUPS WATER

1 CUP UNCOOKED STEEL-CUT OATS

PINCH OF SALT

1 CUP MASHED BANANA

1 TABLESPOON FLAXSEED MEAL

1½ TEASPOONS GROUND CINNAMON

1 TEASPOON VANILLA EXTRACT

½ CUP RAISINS

¼ CUP DRIED CRANBERRIES

1. In a medium saucepan, combine the almond milk and water and bring to a boil.

2. Stir in the oats and salt and reduce the heat to low.

3. Whisk in the mashed banana and flaxseed and simmer for about 20 minutes. Stir the oats every 5 minutes.

4. Remove from the heat and stir in the remaining ingredients.

5. Serve immediately or portion out into containers and store in the fridge.

6. To reheat, add a tablespoon or so of almond milk per serving and warm up in the microwave.

Blueberry Banana Overnight Oats

These overnight oats are the perfect breakfast for busy families. Simply combine the ingredients before you go to bed and it will be ready to serve when you wake up in the morning.

2 CUPS ROLLED OATS

2 CUPS UNSWEETENED ALMOND MILK

¼ CUP PURE MAPLE SYRUP

2 SMALL BANANAS, PEELED AND SLICED

1¼ CUPS FRESH BLUEBERRIES

½ CUP CHOPPED PECANS

2 TABLESPOONS FLAXSEED MEAL

1 TEASPOON GROUND CINNAMON

1 TEASPOON ALMOND EXTRACT

PINCH OF SALT

1. Combine all of the ingredients in a large mixing bowl and stir well.

2. Spoon the mixture into a casserole dish and then cover with plastic and refrigerate overnight.

3. Spoon into bowls in the morning and serve cold, topped with granola if desired.

Raw Buckwheat Porridge

SERVES 4

This raw buckwheat porridge is very easy to customize—simply stir in your favorite spices and top with your favorite dried fruit, nuts, or nut butter.

2 CUPS BUCKWHEAT GROATS

3 TO 4 CUPS WATER

1½ CUPS UNSWEETENED ALMOND MILK

2 TABLESPOONS FLAXSEED MEAL

1 TEASPOON ALMOND EXTRACT

3 TABLESPOONS PURE MAPLE SYRUP

1 TEASPOON GROUND CINNAMON

PINCH OF SALT

½ CUP CHOPPED STRAWBERRIES

1. Place the buckwheat groats in a bowl and cover with the water.

2. Soak the groats overnight and then rinse well and strain.

3. Transfer the groats to a food processor and add the almond milk, flaxseed, and almond extract. Blend the mixture until smooth.

4. Add the maple syrup, ground cinnamon, and salt. Blend smooth.

5. Spoon into bowls and top with chopped strawberries to serve.

Cinnamon Banana Pancakes

SERVES 2 TO 3

If you are a pancake lover, you definitely need to try these cinnamon banana pancakes. Not only are they full of fresh banana flavor, but the moisture in the bananas makes these pancakes soft and tender.

1¼ CUPS WHOLE WHEAT FLOUR

2 TABLESPOONS CANE SUGAR

2 TEASPOONS BAKING POWDER

1½ TEASPOONS GROUND CINNAMON

PINCH OF SALT

DESIRED REPLACEMENT FOR 1 EGG

1 CUP UNSWEETENED ALMOND MILK

1 CUP MASHED BANANA

1. In a mixing bowl, whisk together the flour, sugar, baking powder, cinnamon, and salt.

2. In a small bowl, whisk together the warm water and egg replacer. Let sit for 3 to 5 minutes.

3. Whisk the almond milk into the dry ingredients and then whisk in the egg replacer.

4. Add the mashed banana and then whisk the mixture until smooth.

5. Heat a large nonstick skillet over medium heat.

6. Spoon the batter into the skillet, using 3 to 4 tablespoons per pancake.

7. Cook the pancakes until bubbles form on the surface and then carefully flip them.

8. Continue cooking the pancakes until browned on the underside, about 1 minute more.

9. Transfer the pancakes to a plate and repeat with the remaining batter.

10. Serve hot, drizzled with maple syrup if desired.

Peanut Butter Pancakes

SERVES 3

Pancakes are a quick and easy breakfast that the whole family loves. Feel free to mix up this recipe by substituting almond butter or cashew butter to change the flavor.

1¼ CUPS WHOLE WHEAT FLOUR

2 TABLESPOONS CANE SUGAR

2 TEASPOONS BAKING POWDER

PINCH OF SALT

2 TABLESPOONS WARM WATER

½ TABLESPOON ENER-G EGG REPLACER

1⅓ CUPS UNSWEETENED ALMOND MILK

2 TABLESPOONS SMOOTH PEANUT BUTTER

2 TABLESPOON UNSWEETENED APPLESAUCE

1. In a mixing bowl, whisk together the flour, sugar, baking powder, and salt.

2. In a small bowl, whisk together the warm water and egg replacer.

3. Whisk the almond milk into the dry ingredients and then whisk in the egg replacer mixture.

4. Add the peanut butter and applesauce and whisk the mixture until smooth.

5. Heat a large nonstick skillet over medium heat.

6. Spoon the batter into the skillet, using 3 to 4 tablespoons per pancake.

7. Cook the pancakes until bubbles form on the surface and then carefully flip the pancakes.

8. Continuing cooking the pancakes until browned on the underside, about 1 minute more.

9. Transfer the pancakes to a plate and repeat with the remaining batter.

10. Serve hot, drizzled with maple syrup if desired.

Did you know that some of the foods you have grown up to believe are healthy may have little nutritional value at all? Foods such as cow's milk, eggs, and animal meat are completely devoid of complex carbohydrates and fiber. Even though milk is often cited as a good source of calcium, which is instrumental in preventing osteoporosis, it can actually play a role in leaching calcium from your bones.

Whole Wheat Waffles

SERVES 4

Waffles are a breakfast staple and they are even better when they are home-made. These whole wheat waffles are sure to be a hit with your kids—you may even find yourself making them when your children aren't home so you don't have to share.

1 CUP WHOLE WHEAT FLOUR
3 TABLESPOONS CANE SUGAR
1 TEASPOON BAKING POWDER
PINCH OF SALT
1 CUP UNSWEETENED ALMOND MILK
2 TABLESPOONS CANOLA OIL

1. Preheat waffle iron to high.

2. In a mixing bowl, whisk together the flour, sugar, baking powder, and salt.

3. Whisk in the almond milk and canola oil, stirring until just combined.

4. Pour about ¼ cup of batter into the waffle iron and cook until crisp and lightly browned.

5. Repeat with the remaining batter and serve the waffles hot.

Blueberry Muffins

SERVES 12

There is nothing like waking up to the smell of hot blueberry muffins fresh out of the oven. This will have you wishing every day was Saturday.

1 CUP WHOLE WHEAT FLOUR

¾ CUP UNBLEACHED ALL-PURPOSE FLOUR

¼ CUP WHEAT GERM

1½ TEASPOONS BAKING SODA

PINCH OF SALT

1 CUP UNSWEETENED COCONUT MILK

1 TABLESPOON APPLE CIDER VINEGAR

½ CUP PURE MAPLE SYRUP

¼ CUP MELTED COCONUT OIL

1 TEASPOON VANILLA EXTRACT

1¼ CUPS FRESH BLUEBERRIES

1. Preheat oven to 375°F.

2. Insert paper liners in a 24-cup mini-muffin pan.

3. In a mixing bowl, whisk together the flours, wheat germ, baking soda, and salt.

3. In a small bowl, combine the coconut milk and apple cider vinegar.

4. In a separate bowl, whisk together the maple syrup, coconut oil, and vanilla extract.

5. Gently beat the maple syrup mixture into the dry ingredients and stir until smooth and combined.

6. Whisk in the coconut milk mixture and then fold in the blueberries.

7. Immediately spoon the batter into the prepared muffin pan and bake for 15 to 20 minutes, until a toothpick inserted in the center comes out clean.

8. Cool the muffins for about 10 minutes before serving.

Pumpkin Spice Muffins

SERVES 12

These muffins are the perfect fall breakfast, though you can certainly enjoy them all year round.

1¾ CUPS WHOLE WHEAT FLOUR

¼ CUP GROUND FLAXSEED MEAL

1½ TEASPOONS BAKING SODA

1 TEASPOON GROUND CINNAMON

¼ TEASPOON GROUND NUTMEG

PINCH OF SALT

½ CUP UNSWEETENED COCONUT MILK

1 TABLESPOON APPLE CIDER VINEGAR

½ CUP PURE MAPLE SYRUP

½ CUP PUMPKIN PUREE

¼ CUP MELTED COCONUT OIL

1 TEASPOON ALMOND EXTRACT

1. Preheat oven to 375°F.

2. Insert paper liners in a 24-cup mini-muffin pan.

3. In a large bowl, whisk together the flour, flaxseed, baking soda, cinnamon, nutmeg, and salt.

4. In a small bowl, combine the coconut milk and apple cider vinegar.

5. In a separate bowl, whisk together the maple syrup, pumpkin puree, coconut oil, and almond extract.

6. Gently beat the maple syrup mixture into the dry ingredients and stir until smooth and combined.

7. Whisk in the coconut milk mixture until well combined.

8. Immediately spoon the batter into the prepared muffin pan and bake for 15 to 20 minutes, until a toothpick inserted in the center comes out clean.

9. Cool the muffins for about 10 minutes before serving.

CHAPTER NINE

Dressings, Condiments, and Sauces

Just because you are eliminating meat from your diet doesn't mean you have to give up delicious, flavorful food. The condiments, dressings, and sauces in this chapter will enable you to continue to enjoy your favorite foods, vegan-style. Dip sweet potato fries in your favorite spicy ketchup and sweet barbecue sauce. Spoon basil pesto or cilantro lime sauce onto your sandwiches and wraps. Drizzle freshly made dressings over crisp salads. The options are endless.

RECIPES INCLUDED IN THIS SECTION:

Zesty Citrus Dressing

Apple Cider Dressing

Lemon Sesame Dressing

Raspberry Basil Dressing

Sweet Pear Poppy Seed Dressing

Sun-Dried Tomato Almond Dressing

Creamy Caesar Dressing

Vegan French Dressing

Vegan Italian Dressing

Sweet-and-Sour Dressing

Spicy Tomato Ketchup

Easy Basil Pesto

Sweet Barbecue Sauce

Cilantro Lime Sauce

Cranberry Horseradish Sauce

Roasted Red Pepper Sauce

Tomatillo Sauce

Enchilada Sauce

Adobo Chili Sauce

Spicy Jalapeño Tahini Sauce

Creamy Satay Sauce

Zesty Citrus Dressing

MAKES ABOUT ¼ CUP

This zesty dressing has a light citrus flavor that pairs well with crisp greens. Top your salad with freshly chopped orange or grapefruit to enhance the citrus flavor.

1½ TABLESPOONS LEMON JUICE
1 TABLESPOON LIME JUICE
1 TEASPOON LEMON ZEST
PINCH OF DRY MUSTARD POWDER
¼ CUP EXTRA-VIRGIN OLIVE OIL
¼ CUP GRAPE-SEED OIL

1. In a small bowl, whisk together the lemon juice, lime juice, lemon zest, and mustard powder.

2. While whisking the mixture, drizzle in the olive oil and then the grape-seed oil.

3. Chill until ready to serve.

Apple Cider Dressing

This apple cider dressing has a sweet and unique flavor, perfect for a summer salad topped with fresh fruit.

½ CUP EXTRA-VIRGIN OLIVE OIL
⅓ CUP APPLE CIDER
4 TEASPOONS APPLE CIDER VINEGAR
1 TABLESPOON MINCED WHITE ONION
PINCH OF FRESHLY GROUND BLACK PEPPER

1. In a small bowl, combine all of the ingredients and whisk until smooth and combined.

2. Chill the dressing until ready to serve.

Lemon Sesame Dressing

MAKES ABOUT ¾ CUP

Lemon is known for its fresh flavor and antioxidant properties. This dressing gives you the best of both worlds: flavor and serious health benefits.

¼ CUP TAHINI

2 TABLESPOONS FRESH LEMON JUICE

PINCH OF SALT

PINCH OF FRESHLY GROUND BLACK PEPPER

¼ CUP EXTRA-VIRGIN OLIVE OIL

1 TABLESPOON TOASTED SESAME SEEDS

1. In a medium bowl, whisk the tahini, lemon juice, salt, and pepper until smooth and combined. While whisking, drizzle in the olive oil.

2. Add the sesame seeds and stir until well combined.

Raspberry Basil Dressing

If you are tired of the same old salad dressing, try this raspberry basil dressing. Flavored with dried basil and raspberry vinegar, this dressing will surprise and satisfy.

¼ CUP EXTRA-VIRGIN OLIVE OIL
2 TEASPOONS RASPBERRY VINEGAR
2 TEASPOONS CANE SUGAR
2 TEASPOONS DRIED BASIL
1 TEASPOON GARLIC POWDER
¼ TEASPOON DRY MUSTARD POWDER
PINCH OF SALT
PINCH OF FRESHLY GROUND BLACK PEPPER

1. In a small bowl, combine all of the ingredients and whisk until smooth and combined.

2. Chill the dressing until ready to serve.

Sweet Pear Poppy Seed Dressing

MAKES ABOUT 1 CUP

This sweet dressing is the perfect way to top off a salad made with crisp greens and fresh fruit. A hint of balsamic vinegar and lemon juice set off the sweet flavor of the pear nectar and the fruit itself.

½ RIPE PEAR, PEELED, CORED, AND CHOPPED
⅓ CUP EXTRA-VIRGIN OLIVE OIL
3 TABLESPOONS PEAR NECTAR
1 TABLESPOON BALSAMIC VINEGAR
1 TABLESPOON FRESH LEMON JUICE
PINCH OF SALT
PINCH OF FRESHLY GROUND BLACK PEPPER
1 TABLESPOON POPPY SEEDS

1. Combine all of the ingredients in a blender. Blend until smooth and combined.

2. Chill until ready to use.

. . . .

Try making your own salad dressing using extra-virgin olive oil and balsamic vinegar, or toss fresh greens in lemon juice for a burst of fresh flavor. Don't be afraid to experiment with new flavors, adding a teaspoon of raspberry vinegar or a pinch of dry mustard powder.

. . . .

Sun-Dried Tomato Almond Dressing

MAKES ABOUT 1 CUP

The combination of sun-dried tomatoes and almonds gives this dressing a smooth, unique flavor. Accented with fresh mint and red wine vinegar, this dressing is like nothing you've ever tried before.

½ CUP RAW ALMONDS
⅓ CUP EXTRA-VIRGIN OLIVE OIL
4 SMALL SUN-DRIED TOMATOES IN OIL
3 TABLESPOONS RED WINE VINEGAR
2 TABLESPOONS FRESH CHOPPED MINT LEAVES
PINCH OF SALT
PINCH OF FRESHLY GROUND BLACK PEPPER

1. Combine all of the ingredients in a blender and pulse until smooth and combined. Add more olive oil if the mixture is too thick.

2. Chill the dressing until ready to serve.

Creamy Caesar Dressing

MAKES ABOUT ¾ CUP

This Caesar dressing has all the flavor of its traditional counterpart without the anchovies. Flavored with mustard and lemon juice, this dressing is perfect for tossing with crisp romaine lettuce and red onions.

2 TEASPOONS MINCED GARLIC
1 TABLESPOON VEGAN MUSTARD
1 TABLESPOON DISTILLED WHITE VINEGAR
1 TABLESPOON FRESH LEMON JUICE
PINCH OF SALT
PINCH OF FRESHLY GROUND BLACK PEPPER
½ CUP EXTRA-VIRGIN OLIVE OIL

1. Place the garlic, mustard, vinegar, lemon juice, salt, and pepper in a food processor. Blend the mixture until smooth and combined.

2. With the food processor running, pour in the olive oil.

3. Pour the dressing into a bowl and cover.

4. Chill until ready to serve.

Vegan French Dressing

French dressing was originally a type of vinaigrette, but it has recently come to be known for its sweetness and bright red color. This French dressing is easy to make at home and a great way to add strong flavor to your salads.

½ CUP EXTRA-VIRGIN OLIVE OIL
½ CUP KETCHUP
¼ CUP WHITE WINE VINEGAR
¼ CUP CANE SUGAR
2 TABLESPOONS DRIED ONION
1 TEASPOON GARLIC POWDER
PINCH OF SALT
PINCH OF FRESHLY GROUND BLACK PEPPER

1. Combine all of the ingredients in a blender. Blend until smooth and combined.

2. Chill until ready to use.

Vegan Italian Dressing

MAKES ABOUT 1 CUP

If you prefer the taste of traditional vinaigrette-style salad dressings, this Italian dressing is right up your alley. A combination of red and white wine vinegars mixed with a medley of herbs makes this dressing incredibly flavorful.

2 TABLESPOONS RED WINE VINEGAR

2 TABLESPOONS WHITE WINE VINEGAR

½ TEASPOON DRIED OREGANO

½ TEASPOON DRIED PARSLEY

½ TEASPOON DRIED BASIL

½ TEASPOON SALT

¼ TEASPOON FRESHLY GROUND BLACK PEPPER

¾ CUP EXTRA-VIRGIN OLIVE OIL

1. In a small bowl, whisk together the vinegars and spices.

2. Pour the mixture into a food processor and pulse to blend.

3. With the food processor running, drizzle in the olive oil until well combined.

4. Chill before serving if desired.

Sweet-and-Sour Dressing

This versatile dressing can be used to top salads or as a dipping sauce for fresh vegetables. With just the right combination of sweet and sour, this dressing is sure to please.

⅓ CUP EXTRA-VIRGIN OLIVE OIL
2 TABLESPOONS RICE WINE VINEGAR
2 TABLESPOONS VEGAN PLUM SAUCE
PINCH OF SALT
PINCH OF FRESHLY GROUND BLACK PEPPER

1. Combine all of the ingredients in a blender. Blend until smooth and combined.

2. Chill until ready to use.

Spicy Tomato Ketchup

MAKES ABOUT 2 CUPS

Making your own ketchup at home is not only easier than you might think, but it can also be a great way to experiment with new flavors. Mix in an extra dash of cayenne if you like it hot, or omit it for a more traditional flavor.

2 CUPS DICED TOMATOES
½ CUP VEGETABLE BROTH
1 TABLESPOON APPLE CIDER VINEGAR
1 TABLESPOON BALSAMIC VINEGAR
¼ TEASPOON CAYENNE PEPPER
⅛ TEASPOON GARLIC POWDER
PINCH OF SALT
PINCH OF FRESHLY GROUND BLACK PEPPER

1. In a large bowl, combine all of the ingredients.

2. Puree using an immersion blender until smooth.

3. Store in an airtight container in the refrigerator.

. . . .

Many store-bought ketchups are vegan, although some pack in unnecessary amounts of sugar. Not only does the homemade ketchup above omit the sugar, but it's so flavorful you won't even miss it.

. . . .

Easy Basil Pesto

Pesto is a deliciously fresh spread made from nuts and basil leaves. Spread it on a sandwich or stir it into your favorite pasta.

2 CUPS FRESH BASIL LEAVES, PACKED
½ CUP RAW WALNUT HALVES
1 TEASPOON MINCED GARLIC
½ CUP EXTRA-VIRGIN OLIVE OIL
1 TABLESPOON FRESH LEMON JUICE
2½ TABLESPOONS NUTRITIONAL YEAST
PINCH OF SALT
PINCH OF FRESHLY GROUND BLACK PEPPER

1. In a food processor, combine the basil, walnuts, and garlic. Pulse the mixture to combine, until well ground.

2. With the food processor running, drizzle in the olive oil.

3. Add the remaining ingredients and pulse to blend.

Sweet Barbecue Sauce

This sweet barbecue sauce is the perfect dip for baked sweet potato fries. Try using it as a marinade for grilled portobello mushroom caps.

2 CUPS KETCHUP

3 TABLESPOONS CANE SUGAR

2½ TABLESPOONS LOW-SODIUM SOY SAUCE

2½ TABLESPOONS APPLE CIDER VINEGAR

2 TEASPOONS MINCED GARLIC

PINCH OF DRY MUSTARD POWDER

PINCH OF RED PEPPER FLAKES

1. In a saucepan, combine all of the ingredients over medium heat. Whisk the mixture well and bring to a simmer.

2. Simmer for 15 minutes.

3. Remove from heat and cool to room temperature.

4. Store in an airtight container in the refrigerator.

Cilantro Lime Sauce

This sauce is incredibly creamy and full of fresh cilantro flavor. Serve it as a dipping sauce for chips or drizzle it over black bean tacos.

12 OUNCES FRESH SILKEN TOFU
¼ CUP FRESH CHOPPED CILANTRO LEAVES
1½ TABLESPOONS FRESH LIME JUICE
1 TEASPOON LIME ZEST
PINCH OF SALT
PINCH OF WHITE PEPPER

1. Combine the ingredients in a bowl and stir well.

2. Using an immersion blender, puree the ingredients until well combined.

3. Serve the sauce as a spread for sandwiches or as a topping on burritos.

Cranberry Horseradish Sauce

MAKES ABOUT 1 ½ CUPS

This horseradish sauce is an excellent topping for any dish. Not only does it have the sweet flavor of fresh cranberries, but the horseradish gives it a little kick as well.

10 OUNCES FRESH CRANBERRIES

⅔ CUP WATER

½ CUP CANE SUGAR

⅓ CUP ORANGE JUICE

2 TABLESPOONS FRESH GRATED HORSERADISH

⅛ TEASPOON GROUND GINGER

1. In a small saucepan, stir together the cranberries, water, sugar, orange juice, and horseradish.

2. Bring the mixture to a boil and then reduce the heat to medium-low or low.

3. Simmer the mixture, covered, for about 10 minutes.

4. Remove the cover and cook for another 10 minutes, stirring occasionally.

5. Remove from the heat and stir in the ground ginger.

6. Allow the sauce to cool before serving.

Roasted Red Pepper Sauce

MAKES ABOUT 1 CUP

This sauce is very easy to make and full of flavor. Use it as a spread on sandwiches or stir it into your favorite pasta.

½ CUP ROASTED RED PEPPERS IN OIL
1 MEDIUM PLUM TOMATO, CHOPPED
1 TEASPOON MINCED GARLIC
2 TABLESPOONS RAW WALNUTS
1 TEASPOON RICE WINE VINEGAR
PINCH OF RED PEPPER FLAKES

1. Combine all of the ingredients in a food processor and blend until smooth and combined.

2. Serve the sauce as a dip for vegetables or as a spread for sandwiches.

Tomatillo Sauce

This sauce is just spicy enough to make your taste buds tingle. Serve it with enchiladas, or, if you are feeling adventurous, spread some on your favorite sandwich.

1 POUND TOMATILLOS, HUSKED AND CHOPPED

1 CUP FRESH CILANTRO LEAVES

1 JALAPEÑO PEPPER, CHOPPED

½ RED ONION, CHOPPED

4 TEASPOONS FRESH LIME JUICE

1 TEASPOON MINCED GARLIC

1 TEASPOON OLIVE OIL

½ TEASPOON SALT

1. Combine all of the ingredients in a blender. Pulse the mixture several times and then blend until smooth and combined.

2. Serve the sauce with your favorite Mexican-style dish.

Enchilada Sauce

Homemade enchiladas made with black beans and Mexican rice take on a whole new flavor with this enchilada sauce. If you like your Mexican food spicy, stir in an extra dash of cayenne or a minced jalapeño pepper.

2 TABLESPOONS RICE FLOUR

2 TABLESPOONS CHILI POWDER

2 TEASPOONS GARLIC POWDER

1 TEASPOON GROUND CUMIN

1 TEASPOON DRIED MARJORAM

½ TEASPOON CAYENNE PEPPER

PINCH OF SALT

2 CUPS VEGETABLE BROTH, DIVIDED

1 CUP WATER

2 CUPS TOMATO SAUCE

1. In a medium saucepan, combine the rice flour, spices, and ¼ cup of the vegetable broth. Whisk until a paste forms.

2. Slowly whisk in the remaining vegetable broth and the water.

3. Bring the mixture to a boil over medium heat.

4. Whisk in the tomato sauce and cook for 2 to 3 minutes, until slightly thickened.

5. Remove the saucepan from heat and set aside until ready to use.

Adobo Chili Sauce

MAKES ABOUT 2 CUPS

This sauce is packed with flavor and it's highly versatile. Shake up your mealtime routine by serving it drizzled over steamed vegetables or use it to sauté some peppers and onions for a delicious veggie fajita. Ancho chilies are dried poblano peppers, and they have a sweet, hot flavor.

1 TABLESPOON COCONUT OIL
6 ANCHO CHILIES, DICED
1 TEASPOON MINCED GARLIC
2 CUPS VEGETABLE BROTH
1 TABLESPOON COLD WATER
2 TEASPOONS CORNSTARCH
2 TEASPOONS RICE WINE VINEGAR
PINCH OF SALT
PINCH OF FRESHLY GROUND BLACK PEPPER

1. In a large saucepan, heat the coconut oil over medium heat.

2. Stir in the ancho chilies and garlic and cook for 2 minutes.

3. Whisk in the vegetable broth and bring the mixture to a boil.

4. In a small bowl, whisk together the cold water and cornstarch until smooth. Whisk the mixture into the saucepan. Cook for 2 to 3 minutes, stirring often, until slightly thickened.

5. Stir in the rice wine vinegar, salt, and pepper.

6. Serve the sauce over steamed vegetables or in burritos.

Spicy Jalapeño Tahini Sauce

Tahini is made from ground sesame seeds, and it is an excellent vegan alternative to mayonnaise. Use this tahini sauce as a spread on sandwiches and wraps, or mix it into your favorite homemade hummus.

2 TABLESPOONS CHOPPED JALAPEÑO PEPPER
1 TEASPOON MINCED GARLIC
¼ CUP TAHINI
¼ CUP PLAIN VEGAN YOGURT
3 TABLESPOONS FRESH LEMON JUICE
¼ TEASPOON CAYENNE PEPPER
PINCH OF SALT
PINCH OF FRESHLY GROUND BLACK PEPPER

1. Place the jalapeño and garlic in a food processor and pulse to finely chop.

2. Combine all of the ingredients, including the jalapeño and garlic, in a bowl and stir well.

3. Serve the sauce as a dip for pita chips or as a spread for sandwiches.

Creamy Satay Sauce

MAKES ABOUT 1½ CUPS

Satay is a traditional Indonesian dish consisting of skewered grilled meat served with a peanut-based sauce. Replace the meat with skewered vegetables grilled to perfection and serve them with this creamy sauce.

1 CUP LIGHT COCONUT MILK
¼ CUP SMOOTH PEANUT BUTTER
1 TEASPOON RED CURRY PASTE
PINCH OF SALT

1. In a medium bowl, whisk all of the ingredients together until smooth.

2. Spoon the mixture into a saucepan and heat over medium-low heat until warm.

3. Serve as a dipping sauce or pour over steamed vegetables.

CHAPTER TEN

Salads

If you're new to veganism, you may think your life will be full of unsatisfying salads and raw vegetables. The recipes in this book already prove this notion wrong, and the salads in this chapter will have you looking forward to these sumptuous offerings, whether they're before the main course or *the* main course.

RECIPES INCLUDED IN THIS SECTION:

Tomato Cucumber Summer Salad

Tomato, Corn, and Avocado Salad

Chopped Avocado Salad

Balsamic Sun-Dried Tomato Salad

Arugula, Red Cabbage,
    and Radish Salad

Broccoli Almond Salad

Mandarin Almond Spinach Salad

Strawberry Walnut Salad

Cucumber Apple Pecan Salad

Mixed Berry Mint Salad

Lentil and Tomato Quinoa Salad

Lemon Parsley Orzo Salad

Black Bean, Corn, and Cilantro Salad

Tomato Cucumber Summer Salad

SERVES 6

This summer salad combines the crispness of fresh cucumber with the juiciness of ripe tomatoes. Tossed in a lightly sweetened dressing, this salad is sure to become a family favorite.

4 RIPE TOMATOES, ROUGHLY CHOPPED

1 VIDALIA ONION, SLICED THIN

1 SEEDLESS CUCUMBER, HALVED AND SLICED

2 TABLESPOONS RICE WINE VINEGAR

1 TABLESPOON RED WINE VINEGAR

1 TABLESPOON EXTRA-VIRGIN OLIVE OIL

1 TEASPOON CANE SUGAR

½ TEASPOON SEA SALT

¼ TEASPOON FRESHLY GROUND BLACK PEPPER

¼ CUP CHOPPED FRESH PARSLEY LEAVES

1. In a large bowl, combine the tomatoes, onion, and cucumber.

2. In a small bowl, whisk together the rice wine vinegar, red wine vinegar, olive oil, sugar, salt, and pepper.

3. Drizzle the salad with the vinegar-olive oil mixture and toss to combine.

4. Let the salad stand at room temperature for 30 minutes and then toss with the chopped parsley.

Tomato, Corn, and Avocado Salad

SERVES 4

This fresh and flavorful salad works equally well as an entrée or side dish. Serve it up for family and friends at your next dinner party—or keep a bowl of it in the fridge to enjoy when you need a quick snack.

2 CUPS THAWED FROZEN CORN

2 RIPE PLUM TOMATOES, DICED

1 RIPE AVOCADO, PITTED, PEELED, AND DICED

¼ CUP FRESH CHOPPED CILANTRO LEAVES

2 TABLESPOONS LIME JUICE

SALT TO TASTE

FRESHLY GROUND BLACK PEPPER TO TASTE

1. In a large bowl, combine the corn, tomatoes, and avocado.

2. Add the remaining ingredients and toss to coat.

3. Chill for at least 1 hour before serving.

Chopped Avocado Salad

SERVES ABOUT 6

This chopped avocado salad is the perfect combination of crispy greens and tender avocado. It has so much natural flavor that you don't even need any dressing, although the one provided below is delicious.

4 CUPS CHOPPED ROMAINE LETTUCE

1 CUP HALVED CHERRY TOMATOES

1 SWEET ORANGE PEPPER, SEEDED AND CHOPPED

½ SMALL RED ONION, CHOPPED

3 TABLESPOONS FRESH LIME JUICE

3 TABLESPOONS FRESH LEMON JUICE

2 TABLESPOONS EXTRA-VIRGIN OLIVE OIL

½ TEASPOON SEA SALT

¼ TEASPOON GROUND CUMIN

1 RIPE AVOCADO, PEELED AND PITTED

FRESHLY GROUND BLACK PEPPER TO TASTE

1. In a large bowl, combine the lettuce, tomatoes, orange pepper, and red onion. Toss well.

2. In a small bowl, whisk together the lime juice, lemon juice, olive oil, sea salt, and cumin.

3. Add the dressing to the salad and toss to coat.

4. Chop the avocado and spread it on top of the salad.

5. Serve with freshly ground black pepper.

Balsamic Sun-Dried Tomato Salad

SERVES 2

Sun-dried tomatoes have a deep, rich flavor that is offset nicely by fresh balsamic vinegar in this recipe. Serve this salad to your friends for lunch or use it as a side dish for dinner.

4 CUPS BABY SPINACH LEAVES
2 CUPS CHOPPED ROMAINE LETTUCE
1 CUP HALVED CHERRY TOMATOES
¼ CUP THINLY SLICED RED ONION
2 SUN-DRIED TOMATOES IN OIL, DRAINED
2 TABLESPOONS EXTRA-VIRGIN OLIVE OIL
2 TABLESPOONS BALSAMIC VINEGAR
1 TEASPOON MINCED GARLIC
FRESHLY GROUND BLACK PEPPER TO TASTE

1. In a large bowl, toss the spinach, lettuce, cherry tomatoes, and red onion.

2. Combine the remaining ingredients (except for the black pepper) in a food processor. Pulse twice and then blend until smooth and well combined.

3. Drizzle the dressing over the salad and toss to coat.

4. Divide the salad between two bowls, garnish with freshly ground black pepper, and serve.

Arugula, Red Cabbage, and Radish Salad

SERVES 4

Radishes are known for their anti-cancer properties as well as their high vitamin C content. Combined with fresh arugula and red cabbage, this salad has a bold and unique flavor.

2 CUPS THINLY SLICED RADISHES
¼ CUP CHOPPED BASIL LEAVES
4 CUPS FRESH ARUGULA
2 CUPS THINLY SLICED RED CABBAGE
¼ CUP FRESH LEMON JUICE
3 TABLESPOON EXTRA-VIRGIN OLIVE OIL
1 TABLESPOON WHITE WINE VINEGAR
PINCH OF SEA SALT

1. In a large bowl, combine the radishes and basil leaves. Stir well.

2. Add the arugula and red cabbage and toss well.

3. In a small bowl, whisk together the lemon juice, olive oil, vinegar, and salt.

4. Add the dressing to the salad, toss well to coat the salad, and serve immediately.

Broccoli Almond Salad

This broccoli almond salad is perfect for a summer picnic or just as a quick, refreshing meal. Made with fresh vegetables and tossed in a lightly sweetened dressing, this salad is sure to please.

6 CUPS CHOPPED BROCCOLI FLORETS

1 LARGE STALK CELERY, DICED

1 PEELED CARROT, DICED

⅓ CUP TAHINI

3 TABLESPOONS PURE MAPLE SYRUP

1 TABLESPOON EXTRA-VIRGIN OLIVE OIL

1 TABLESPOON FRESH LEMON JUICE

¼ CUP THINLY SLICED GREEN ONIONS

½ CUP THINLY SLICED ALMONDS

1. Combine the broccoli, celery, and carrots in a bowl. Stir well.

2. Place the tahini, maple syrup, olive oil, and lemon juice in a bowl and whisk until smooth and combined.

3. Pour the dressing over the salad and toss to coat.

4. Toss with the green onions and sliced almonds just before serving.

Mandarin Almond Spinach Salad

SERVES 2

Baby spinach is loaded with vitamins, and it is also known for its high levels of calcium and iron. You may also be surprised to find that spinach is a good source of vegetarian protein; combined with almonds, this salad packs a protein-filled punch.

4 CUPS FRESH BABY SPINACH
1 SMALL CAN MANDARIN ORANGES, DRAINED
¼ SMALL RED ONION, SLICED THIN
¼ CUP SLICED ALMONDS

1. Combine the spinach, oranges, and red onion in a salad bowl. Toss to combine.

2. Divide between two bowls, and top each salad with sliced almonds and your favorite dressing just before serving.

. . . .

Although you don't need to avoid them completely, be wary of canned and preserved fruits and vegetables. Even though they may be vegan, they might not be as healthy as you think. Processed and canned produce are often high in sodium, so it is better to opt for fresh or all natural, frozen veggies. If you do buy canned products, rinse and strain them under cool water before using them to reduce the level of sodium.

. . . .

Strawberry Walnut Salad

This delicious salad combines the flavors of fresh fruit and nuts to perfection. Feel free to swap out your favorite nuts and berries if strawberries and walnuts aren't for you.

2 CUPS FRESH SPRING GREENS

4 SLICED STRAWBERRIES

½ CUP THINLY SLICED RED CABBAGE

4 THIN SLICES RED ONION

2 TABLESPOONS CHOPPED WALNUTS

1. In a large bowl, toss the greens, strawberries, and red cabbage.

2. Top the salad with the red onion and sprinkle with chopped walnuts.

3. Serve immediately with your favorite dressing.

Cucumber Apple Pecan Salad

SERVES 3 TO 4

If you are looking for a quick and refreshing salad, look no further than this cucumber apple pecan salad. Packed with dietary fiber and fresh flavor, this salad is sure to satisfy.

8 CUPS FRESH BABY GREENS

2 CRISP APPLES, CORED AND SLICED THIN

1 SEEDLESS CUCUMBER, SLICED THIN

2 TABLESPOONS FRESH LEMON JUICE

½ TABLESPOON FRESH LIME JUICE

½ TABLESPOON ORGANIC RED WINE VINEGAR

3 TABLESPOONS CHOPPED PECANS

3 TABLESPOONS DRIED CRANBERRIES

1. In a large bowl, combine the greens, apple, and cucumber.

2. Add the lemon juice, lime juice, and red wine vinegar, and toss to coat the salad.

3. Divide the salad among bowls or plates and top each serving with chopped pecans and dried cranberries.

Mixed Berry Mint Salad

SERVES 3 TO 4

In this fruit salad, mixed berries blend well with the fresh flavor of mint. Serve this fruit salad as a snack or enjoy it for breakfast any day of the week.

2 CUPS HALVED STRAWBERRIES
1½ CUPS BLUEBERRIES
1 CUP RASPBERRIES
1 CUP BLACKBERRIES
½ CUP CHOPPED FRESH MINT LEAVES
2 TABLESPOONS FRESH LIME JUICE

1. Combine the berries in a large bowl.

2. Add the mint leaves and lime juice and toss to coat.

3. Transfer to a serving bowl and chill before serving, if desired.

Lentil and Tomato Quinoa Salad

SERVES 4

Packed with protein as well as flavor, this lentil and tomato quinoa salad can be enjoyed as either a meal or side dish. Make up a big batch and enjoy it all week long.

3 CUPS WATER, DIVIDED
½ CUP DRIED QUINOA
½ CUP DRIED RED LENTILS
3 TABLESPOONS EXTRA-VIRGIN OLIVE OIL
2 TABLESPOONS RED WINE VINEGAR
1 TABLESPOON FRESH LEMON JUICE
3 TABLESPOONS FRESH CHOPPED CILANTRO
4 CUPS CHOPPED ROMAINE LETTUCE
¼ CUP THINLY SLICED GREEN ONION

1. Place the quinoa in a mesh sieve and run under cold water for 2 minutes, swishing the quinoa with your hand.

2. Transfer the quinoa to small saucepan and add 1 cup water.

3. Bring the quinoa to a boil and then reduce heat and simmer for 15 minutes, until the quinoa absorbs the water. Remove from heat to cool.

4. Rinse the lentils under fresh water and then place them in a medium saucepan with 2 cups water.

5. Bring the lentils to a boil and then reduce heat and simmer for 30 minutes, covered.

6. Drain the lentils and set aside to cool.

7. In a small bowl, whisk together the olive oil, vinegar, lemon juice, and cilantro to make a dressing.

8. Combine the cooled quinoa and lentils in a serving bowl with the chopped romaine lettuce.

9. Toss the salad to coat with the dressing and then chill for 20 minutes.

10. Garnish with sliced green onions to serve.

. . . .

Make your salads and stir-fries more filling by adding chewy foods that require more time and effort to eat. Try some sautéed tofu, grilled mushrooms, or toasted nuts.

. . . .

Lemon Parsley Orzo Salad

Cool and refreshing, this lemon parsley orzo salad is the perfect dish to share at your next family gathering or summer picnic.

2 CUPS DRIED ORZO PASTA

¼ CUP EXTRA-VIRGIN OLIVE OIL

¼ CUP FRESH LEMON JUICE

2 TABLESPOONS APPLE CIDER VINEGAR

1 TABLESPOON LEMON ZEST

1 CUP HALVED CHERRY TOMATOES

1 STALK CELERY, DICED

½ SMALL RED ONION, DICED

½ SEEDLESS CUCUMBER, DICED

½ CUP FRESH CHOPPED PARSLEY LEAVES

SEA SALT TO TASTE

FRESHLY GROUND BLACK PEPPER TO TASTE

1. Bring a pot of water to boil and add the orzo. Cook until tender, about 8 to 10 minutes. Stir occasionally.

2. Drain the orzo and rinse in cool water. Set aside in a large bowl.

3. In a small bowl, whisk together the olive oil, lemon juice, vinegar, and lemon zest.

4. Stir the tomatoes, celery, red onion, cucumber, and parsley into the bowl with the orzo.

5. Stir in the olive oil mixture and toss to coat. Season with salt and pepper and serve immediately.

Black Bean, Corn, and Cilantro Salad

Looking for something with a little bit of Mexican flair? This black bean, corn, and cilantro salad is the perfect combination of high-fiber foods, flavored with the refreshing taste of cilantro.

2 (15-OUNCE) CANS BLACK BEANS, RINSED AND DRAINED

2½ CUPS THAWED FROZEN CORN

1 MEDIUM RIPE TOMATO, DICED

½ SMALL RED ONION, SLICED THIN

½ CUP FRESH CHOPPED CILANTRO LEAVES

¼ CUP FRESH LEMON JUICE

1 TABLESPOON FRESH LIME JUICE

2 TEASPOONS PURE MAPLE SYRUP

½ TEASPOON SEA SALT

¼ TEASPOON FRESHLY GROUND BLACK PEPPER

1. In a large serving bowl, toss together the beans, corn, tomato, red onion, and cilantro.

2. In a small bowl, whisk together the remaining ingredients.

3. Drizzle the dressing over the salad and toss to coat. Serve immediately.

CHAPTER ELEVEN

Side Dishes and Appetizers

In this chapter you will find a wide variety of delicious yet simple vegan side dishes and appetizers. Having the right dish to serve before or alongside your main entrée is the key to successful meal planning. A side dish can complement the ingredients or flavors in your main entrée, or it can act as a contrast, while an appetizer can whet the appetite for what is yet to come.

RECIPES INCLUDED IN THIS SECTION:

Spicy Tomato Salsa

Black Bean and Corn Salsa

Mango Citrus Salsa

Roasted Garlic Hummus

White Bean Hummus

Avocado Lime Hummus

Spicy Guacamole

Corn Pudding

Sweet Asian Coleslaw

Easy Mexican Rice

Refried Beans

Baked Sweet Potato Fries

Baked Eggplant Fries

Sautéed Spinach with Garlic

Braised Bok Choy with Ginger

Acorn Squash Pilaf

Maple Ginger Brussels Sprouts

Steamed Sesame Coconut Broccolini

Spicy Tomato Salsa

This spicy tomato salsa is a snap to throw together. If you have time to prepare it in advance, however, the flavor will intensify the longer you chill it in the refrigerator.

1 POUND FRESH STEM TOMATOES

½ GREEN BELL PEPPER, SEEDED AND DICED

½ RED BELL PEPPER, SEEDED AND DICED

¼ SMALL RED ONION, DICED

1 JALAPEÑO PEPPER, SEEDED AND MINCED

1 CLOVE GARLIC, MINCED

2 TEASPOONS GROUND CUMIN

1 TEASPOON SALT

⅛ TEASPOON CAYENNE PEPPER

1. Trim the tomatoes to remove the stems and chop them coarsely into a bowl.

2. Stir in the diced peppers and onion along with the jalapeño pepper.

3. Add the garlic, cumin, salt, and cayenne and stir well to combine.

4. Cover the bowl and chill for several hours to allow the flavors to combine before serving.

5. Serve cold with chips for dipping.

Black Bean and Corn Salsa

This salsa makes an excellent snack or appetizer. Serve it with chips for dipping or roll it up into a fresh corn tortilla.

1 (14.5 OUNCE) CAN BLACK BEANS
2 CUPS THAWED FROZEN CORN
½ SWEET RED PEPPER, DICED
2 GREEN ONIONS, CHOPPED
2 TABLESPOONS EXTRA-VIRGIN OLIVE OIL
2 TABLESPOONS LIME JUICE
1 TEASPOON GROUND CUMIN
PINCH OF SALT
PINCH OF FRESHLY GROUND BLACK PEPPER

1. Rinse and drain the black beans and then place them in a mixing bowl.

2. Add the corn, red pepper, and green onions and stir until well combined.

3. In a small bowl, whisk together the remaining ingredients.

4. Pour the dressing over the black beans and vegetables, and toss to coat.

5. Chill until ready to serve.

Mango Citrus Salsa

SERVES 6

This mango citrus salsa works equally well as a side dish, an appetizer, or as a topping for your favorite salad. Serve it up cold and discover just how well the flavors of mango and citrus fruit combine.

2 RIPE MANGOES, PEELED, PITTED, AND CHOPPED
1 RIPE ORANGE, PEELED AND CHOPPED
1 RIPE TANGERINE, PEELED AND CHOPPED
¼ CUP FRESH CHOPPED CILANTRO LEAVES
2 TABLESPOONS MINCED RED ONION
2 TABLESPOONS FRESH LEMON JUICE
1 TEASPOON FRESH LEMON ZEST
PINCH OF SALT
PINCH OF FRESHLY GROUND BLACK PEPPER

1. In a serving bowl, add the chopped mango, orange, tangerine, cilantro, and red onion. Toss to combine.

2. Drizzle the lemon juice over the ingredients and then add the lemon zest, salt, and pepper.

3. Toss until the fruit is well coated, then cover and chill overnight before serving cold.

Roasted Garlic Hummus

MAKES ABOUT 1½ CUPS

Roasted garlic hummus is the perfect party snack. Full of flavor, this hummus is the ideal dip for chips or fresh vegetable sticks.

2 CUPS DRIED CHICKPEAS

½ CUP RAW CASHEWS

¼ CUP EXTRA-VIRGIN OLIVE OIL

2 TABLESPOONS FRESH LEMON JUICE

2 TABLESPOONS WATER

2 TABLESPOONS ROASTED GARLIC

1 TEASPOON SALT

1. Place the chickpeas in a bowl and cover with water. Soak the chickpeas overnight, replacing the water once.

2. Drain the chickpeas and place them in a food processor with the remaining ingredients.

3. Blend the mixture until smooth and combined.

4. Transfer to a bowl and chill if desired before serving.

White Bean Hummus

A unique twist on traditional hummus, this white bean hummus makes a great appetizer. Serve it with chips or fresh veggies for dipping.

2 CUPS DRIED CANNELLINI BEANS

½ CUP RAW CASHEWS

¼ CUP EXTRA-VIRGIN OLIVE OIL

2 TABLESPOONS WATER

2 TABLESPOONS FRESH LEMON JUICE

1 CLOVE GARLIC, PEELED

1 TEASPOON SALT

1. Place the beans in a bowl and cover with water.

2. Soak the beans overnight, replacing the water once.

3. Drain the beans and place them in a food processor with the remaining ingredients.

4. Blend the mixture until smooth and combined.

5. Chill if desired before serving.

Avocado Lime Hummus

If you are a fan of hummus, you definitely need to try this recipe. The flavor of traditional chickpea hummus blends perfectly with accents of avocado and lime for a refreshing appetizer or snack.

2 CUPS DRIED CHICKPEAS

1 RIPE AVOCADO, PEELED AND PITTED

½ CUP RAW CASHEWS

¼ CUP EXTRA-VIRGIN OLIVE OIL

2 TABLESPOONS FRESH LIME JUICE

2 TABLESPOONS WATER

1 CLOVE GARLIC, PEELED

1 TEASPOON SALT

1. Place the chickpeas in a bowl and cover with water. Soak the chickpeas overnight, replacing the water once.

2. Drain the chickpeas and place them in a food processor with the remaining ingredients.

3. Blend the mixture until smooth and combined.

4. Transfer to a bowl and chill if desired before serving.

Spicy Guacamole

MAKES ABOUT 1½ CUPS

If you are looking for a quick and easy snack or appetizer to whip up for friends and family, this spicy guacamole is a great option. Made with ripe avocados, tomato, and jalapeño, this guacamole is made for dipping.

2 RIPE AVOCADOS, PEELED AND PITTED

1 RIPE TOMATO, CORED AND DICED

1 JALAPEÑO PEPPER, SEEDED AND MINCED

1 CLOVE GARLIC, MINCED

1 TABLESPOON FRESH LIME JUICE

¼ TEASPOON CHILI POWDER

¼ TEASPOON GROUND CUMIN

PINCH OF SALT

1. Spoon the avocado into a mixing bowl and add the tomato.

2. Stir in the jalapeño and garlic, mashing the mixture together with the back of a fork.

3. Add the remaining ingredients and stir until well combined.

4. Chill for at least 1 hour before serving.

Corn Pudding

This corn pudding is guaranteed to be a family favorite. Made with fresh corn kernels, rice flour, and coconut milk, this recipe uses only the freshest, most wholesome ingredients.

COOKING SPRAY

3 EARS FRESH YELLOW CORN, HUSKED

2 TABLESPOONS WHITE RICE FLOUR

2 TABLESPOONS CANE SUGAR

2 TABLESPOONS COCONUT OIL

½ CUP PLAIN VEGAN YOGURT

SALT TO TASTE

FRESHLY GROUND BLACK PEPPER TO TASTE

1 CUP UNSWEETENED COCONUT MILK

PREHEAT OVEN TO 325°F.

LIGHTLY OIL A 2-QUART CASSEROLE DISH.

1. Preheat oven to 325°F.

2. Lightly oil a 2-quart casserole dish. Then 3. Slice the kernels...

3. Slice the kernels off the corn cobs into a medium bowl. Discard the cobs.

4. In a blender, combine ½ cup of the corn kernels with the rice flour, cane sugar, coconut oil, yogurt, salt, and pepper. Blend the mixture until smooth and well combined.

5. Pour the mixture into the prepared dish and stir in the coconut milk and the remaining corn kernels.

6. Bake the mixture for 40 to 45 minutes, until the center is set.

7. Cool for 10 minutes before serving.

Sweet Asian Coleslaw

Cabbage is an excellent natural source of vitamin E, and it also contains sulfur, which helps detox the liver. Combined with the health benefits of carrots, onion, and cilantro, this recipe is lightly sweet and highly refreshing.

4 CUPS CHINESE CABBAGE, SLICED THIN

1 CUP SHREDDED CARROTS

¼ CUP DICED RED ONION

¼ CUP CHOPPED CILANTRO LEAVES

1 TABLESPOON RICE WINE VINEGAR

1 TABLESPOON CANOLA OIL

1 TABLESPOON SESAME OIL

1 TEASPOON SUGAR

PINCH OF SALT

1. In a large bowl, add the cabbage, carrot, red onion and cilantro. Mix by hand until well combined.

2. In a small bowl, whisk together the remaining ingredients.

3. Pour over the vegetables and toss to coat.

4. Cover and chill for 1 hour before serving.

Easy Mexican Rice

SERVES 4 TO 5

This rice is incredibly easy to prepare and it is simple to multiply the recipe to feed a crowd. Use this as a side dish for your favorite meal, or scoop it into fresh corn tortillas along with some refried beans. Use the Adobo Chili recipe from Chapter 10 to make this dish completely homemade.

1 VERY LARGE RIPE PLUM TOMATO
1 MEDIUM VIDALIA ONION, COARSELY CHOPPED
1½ TABLESPOONS EXTRA-VIRGIN OLIVE OIL
2 TEASPOONS MINCED GARLIC
2 JALAPEÑO PEPPERS, SEEDED AND MINCED
¼ CUP PLUS 1 TABLESPOON VEGETABLE BROTH
½ CUP WATER
1 TABLESPOON ADOBO CHILI SAUCE
1⅔ CUPS QUICK-COOKING BROWN RICE
SALT TO TASTE
FRESHLY GROUND BLACK PEPPER TO TASTE

1. Combine the tomato and onion in a blender and blend until smooth and pureed.

2. In a medium saucepan, heat the oil over medium-high heat. Add the garlic and jalapeño and cook for about 1 minute, stirring often.

3. Stir in the tomato-onion mixture along with the vegetable broth, water, and adobo chili sauce.

4. Bring the mixture to a boil, then stir in the brown rice.

5. Reduce the heat until the mixture is at a slow boil and cook for 12 to 15 minutes, until the rice has absorbed most of the liquid.

6. Season with salt and pepper to taste.

7. Let the rice sit, covered, for 5 minutes before serving.

Refried Beans

SERVES 4 TO 5

These refried beans are a wonderful dish to prepare for a crowd. You can make the beans a day or two ahead of time and then simply reheat them with a little oil, water, and adobo chili sauce. Use the Adobo Chili recipe from Chapter 10 to make this dish completely homemade.

3½ CUPS COOKED PINTO BEANS
3 CUPS VEGETABLE BROTH
2 TABLESPOONS ADOBO CHILI SAUCE, DIVIDED
1 TABLESPOON COCONUT OIL
1 OR 2 CLOVES GARLIC, MINCED
½ CUP WATER
SALT TO TASTE
FRESHLY GROUND BLACK PEPPER TO TASTE

1. In a saucepan, combine the pinto beans, vegetable broth, and 1 tablespoon of adobo chili sauce.

2. Bring the mixture to a boil and then reduce the heat and simmer for 10 minutes.

3. Set the beans aside for 10 minutes. (You can also prepare the beans 1 or 2 days in advance.)

4. In a heavy skillet, heat the coconut oil over medium-high heat. Add the garlic and the remaining adobo chili sauce and cook for 1 minute.

5. Stir in the cooked beans along with the water.

6. Reduce the heat and simmer the mixture for 5 to 10 minutes, stirring and mashing the beans with a wooden spoon.

7. Season with salt and pepper to taste and serve hot.

Baked Sweet Potato Fries

SERVES 4 TO 6

If you are tired of traditional French fries, these sweet potato fries might just surprise you. Lightly sweet and tender, with a crispy outside, these are a sure palate pleaser.

3 LARGE SWEET POTATOES
¼ CUP EXTRA-VIRGIN OLIVE OIL
1 TABLESPOON SEA SALT
1 TABLESPOON CANE SUGAR (OPTIONAL)
1 TABLESPOON CHILI POWDER

1. Preheat oven to 450°F.

2. Cut the sweet potatoes into wedges or ½-inch strips as desired.

3. Place the sweet potatoes in a large bowl and add the olive oil, salt, sugar, and chili powder. Toss to coat.

4. Arrange the sweet potatoes on a rimmed baking sheet and bake for 15 minutes.

5. Carefully flip the fries and bake for 10 to 15 minutes longer, until browned.

6. Cool for 5 minutes before serving.

Baked Eggplant Fries

Eggplant fries are a delicious alternative to standard potato or sweet potato fries. Serve these hot with your favorite sauce for dipping.

1 POUND EGGPLANT
1¼ CUPS UNBLEACHED ALL-PURPOSE OR ALMOND FLOUR
½ TEASPOON SEASONING SALT
1 CUP UNSWEETENED COCONUT MILK

1. Preheat oven to 425°F.

2. Line a baking sheet with parchment paper.

3. Carefully peel the eggplant with a sharp knife. Then cut it into ½-inch-thick strips and set them aside.

4. In a shallow dish, stir together the flour and salt.

5. Pour the coconut milk into another shallow dish.

6. Dip the fries, several at a time, into the coconut milk and then dredge with the flour mixture.

7. Arrange the coated fries on the baking sheet and bake for 10 to 15 minutes.

8. Flip the fries and bake for another 10 to 15 minutes, until lightly browned and crisp around the edges.

Sautéed Spinach with Garlic

SERVES 4

This sautéed spinach is a very versatile recipe, and it can be served with almost any entrée. If you are in a hurry, or simply don't know what to make for dinner, whip up a quick batch of this and enjoy.

1 TABLESPOON COCONUT OIL
1 TABLESPOON MINCED GARLIC
1 LARGE BUNCH FRESH BABY SPINACH
PINCH OF SALT

1. Heat the oil in a skillet over medium heat.

2. Add the garlic and cook for 1 minute.

3. Stir in the spinach and cook for 2 to 3 minutes, until wilted.

4. Season with salt and serve hot.

. . . .

Did you know that you can reduce the number of calories you cook with by swapping out oil or butter for reduced-sodium vegetable broth? Just a few tablespoons are all you need for sautéing vegetables to serve with pasta, salad, or steamed rice.

. . . .

Braised Bok Choy with Ginger

SERVES 4

Bok choy is a leafy Chinese cabbage rich in a number of essential vitamins and minerals, as well antioxidants, which gives it cholesterol-reducing and cancer-fighting power.

1 TABLESPOON EXTRA-VIRGIN OLIVE OIL

1 TABLESPOON FRESH GRATED GINGERROOT

1 TEASPOON MINCED GARLIC

2 TABLESPOONS WATER

1 TEASPOON CORNSTARCH

½ TABLESPOON FRESH LEMON JUICE

1 POUND FRESH BOK CHOY, CHOPPED

SALT TO TASTE

FRESHLY GROUND BLACK PEPPER TO TASTE

1. Heat the oil in a large skillet over medium heat.

2. Add the ginger and garlic and cook for about 1 minute.

3. In a small bowl, whisk together the water, cornstarch, and lemon juice.

4. Stir the bok choy into the skillet and cook for 2 minutes, until it begins to soften.

5. Stir in the water and cornstarch mixture, cover the skillet, and cook for about 2 minutes.

6. Remove from the heat and season with salt and pepper to serve.

Acorn Squash Pilaf

SERVES 6 TO 8

This acorn squash pilaf is relatively simple to make but full of unique flavor. Don't be afraid to try this recipe with other types of squash, such as butternut squash or even pumpkin.

2 POUNDS FRESH ACORN SQUASH

2 TABLESPOONS EXTRA-VIRGIN OLIVE OIL

1 TEASPOON MINCED GARLIC

1 SMALL RED ONION, DICED

2 TABLESPOONS WARM WATER

1 TABLESPOON TOMATO PASTE

1 CUP INSTANT BROWN RICE

1½ CUPS VEGETABLE BROTH

½ CUP VEGAN DRY WHITE WINE

1 TEASPOON SALT

PINCH OF GROUND NUTMEG

1. Cut the squash in half and carefully remove the peel using a sharp knife.

2. Scoop the seeds out and discard them, and then grate the squash into a large bowl.

3. In a heavy skillet, heat the olive oil over medium-high heat and stir in the garlic. Cook for 1 minute, and then stir in the onion.

4. Cook, stirring, for 6 to 8 minutes until the onions begin to soften.

5. In a small bowl, whisk together the water and tomato paste, and then stir the mixture into the skillet.

6. Add the instant brown rice and stir the mixture well.

7. Stir in the grated squash and cook the mixture until the squash has cooked down enough that you can cover the skillet.

8. Bring the mixture to a simmer and stir in the vegetable broth and wine. Cover the skillet and bring the mixture to a boil.

9. Reduce the heat and simmer the mixture for 20 to 25 minutes, until the rice and squash are tender.

10. Stir in the salt and nutmeg and let sit for about 5 minutes before serving.

Maple Ginger Brussels Sprouts

SERVES 6

Brussels sprouts are incredibly high in dietary fiber and they are also a good source of potassium and manganese. A single serving of Brussels sprouts contains more vitamin K and vitamin C than you need for an entire day.

1 POUND BRUSSELS SPROUTS, TRIMMED AND QUARTERED
½ TABLESPOON PURE MAPLE SYRUP
½ TEASPOON SESAME OIL
½ TEASPOON SALT
1 TABLESPOON BALSAMIC VINEGAR
1 TEASPOON EXTRA-VIRGIN OLIVE OIL
1 TABLESPOON FRESH MINCED OR GRATED GINGERROOT
1 CLOVE GARLIC, MINCED

1. Place a steamer pan inside a saucepan and add about 1 inch of water.

2. Place the Brussels sprouts in the pan and steam for about 5 minutes, until tender.

3. In a small bowl, whisk together the maple syrup, sesame oil, salt, and balsamic vinegar.

4. In a large saucepan, heat the olive oil over medium-high heat. Add the ginger and garlic and cook for about 1 minute.

5. Stir in the maple syrup mixture and cook for 1 minute more.

6. Add the Brussels sprouts and toss to coat with the sauce. Serve hot.

Steamed Sesame Coconut Broccolini

Broccolini is very similar to broccoli in both taste and appearance, but it has smaller florets and thinner stalks. The best way to serve this delicious vegetable is lightly steamed, tossed in a flavorful dressing.

1 POUND FRESH BROCCOLINI

2 TABLESPOONS COCONUT OIL

1 TEASPOON DARK SESAME OIL

1 TABLESPOON RED WINE VINEGAR

2 TABLESPOONS PINEAPPLE JUICE

½ TEASPOON GARLIC POWDER

1 TABLESPOON TOASTED SESAME SEEDS (OPTIONAL)

1. Place a steamer insert in a large saucepan and fill the pan with about ½ to 1 inch of water.

2. Place the broccolini in the steamer insert and steam, covered, for 3 to 5 minutes, until tender.

3. In a large bowl, whisk together the oils, vinegar, pineapple juice, and garlic powder.

4. Add the steamed broccolini to the bowl and toss to coat.

5. Transfer the broccolini to a serving dish and sprinkle with toasted sesame seeds to serve.

CHAPTER TWELVE

Soups and Stews

Having a wide variety of soup and stew recipes on hand is essential for living a healthy vegan lifestyle. They are a great way to fuel your body with vital nutrients, and it is also easy to make multiple servings so you have a meal that lasts several days. The recipes you will find in this chapter utilize a variety of healthy ingredients from cauliflower and avocado to lentils, red beans, and nuts.

RECIPES INCLUDED IN THIS SECTION:

Roasted Tomato Basil Soup

Roasted Leek and Potato Soup

Spicy Mushroom Spinach Soup

Curried Lentil Soup

Asian Vegetable Soup

Creamy Cauliflower Soup

Tomato Gazpacho

Chilled Watermelon Soup

Cold "Cream" of Asparagus Soup

Creamy Cold Avocado Soup

Sweet Potato Carrot Stew

Chickpea Butternut Squash Stew

Garlic Red Bean Stew

Curried Vegetable Stew

Roasted Tomato Basil Soup

SERVES 4 TO 6

There is just something about homemade tomato soup that makes any place feel like home. This roasted tomato basil soup is unlike anything you will ever eat from a can.

2½ POUNDS RIPE TOMATOES

2 YELLOW ONIONS, SLICED THIN

2 TABLESPOONS MINCED GARLIC

1 CUP CHOPPED BASIL LEAVES, PLUS EXTRA FOR GARNISHING

3 TABLESPOONS EXTRA-VIRGIN OLIVE OIL

SALT TO TASTE

FRESHLY GROUND BLACK PEPPER TO TASTE

1 CUP VEGETABLE BROTH

½ CUP CANNED COCONUT MILK (OPTIONAL)

1. Preheat oven to 450°F.

2. Cut the tomatoes in half and spread them cut-side up on a rimmed baking sheet.

3. Sprinkle the onions, garlic, and chopped basil on top of the tomatoes.

4. Drizzle with olive oil and season with salt and pepper.

5. Roast the vegetables for 20 to 25 minutes, until the onions are caramelized and the tomatoes slightly charred.

6. Scoop the vegetables into a large stockpot and add the vegetable broth. Bring to a boil.

7. Remove from heat and puree the soup with an immersion blender.

continued ▶

8. Whisk in the coconut milk, if using, and return the soup to the heat.

9. Cook until heated through and then serve hot, garnished with fresh basil leaves.

. . . .

Add some texture and body to your favorite soups and sauces by using pureed vegetables instead of milk or cream. Not only will this up the fiber content of the dish, but it will also help you to keep the calorie count down.

. . . .

Roasted Leek and Potato Soup

SERVES 6

Leeks are full of healthy vitamins, minerals, and antioxidants. In this recipe, the flavors of roasted leek and potato mesh perfectly in a hearty soup.

2 POUNDS YUKON GOLD POTATOES, QUARTERED

2 LEEKS, RINSED AND CHOPPED (WHITE AND LIGHT GREEN PARTS ONLY)

3 TABLESPOONS EXTRA-VIRGIN OLIVE OIL, DIVIDED

1 TABLESPOON MINCED GARLIC

1 LARGE YELLOW ONION, CHOPPED

5 CUPS LOW-SODIUM VEGETABLE BROTH

1 TEASPOON SALT

½ TEASPOON FRESHLY GROUND BLACK PEPPER

1 CUP UNSWEETENED COCONUT MILK

1. Preheat oven to 375°F.

2. In a large bowl, add the potatoes, leeks, 2 tablespoons oil, and garlic, and toss to coat.

3. Spread the potatoes and leeks on a rimmed baking sheet and roast for 30 to 40 minutes, until lightly charred.

4. In a stockpot, heat the remaining tablespoon olive oil over medium heat.

5. Stir in the onions and cook until tender, about 5 minutes.

6. Add the roasted potatoes and leeks and stir well.

7. Stir in the vegetable broth, salt, and pepper.

8. Bring the soup to a boil and then remove from heat and puree using an immersion blender.

9. Whisk in the coconut milk and serve hot.

Spicy Mushroom Spinach Soup

The flavors of fresh mushroom and garlic blend perfectly in this hot soup, offset by the subtle taste and texture of wilted spinach.

1 TABLESPOON COCONUT OIL

1 TEASPOON MINCED GARLIC

2 POUNDS FRESH MUSHROOMS, CHOPPED

1 LARGE YELLOW ONION, CHOPPED

5 CUPS LOW-SODIUM VEGETABLE BROTH

3 CUPS BABY SPINACH LEAVES

½ TEASPOON SALT

¼ TEASPOON FRESHLY GROUND BLACK PEPPER

1. In a stockpot, heat the oil over medium-high heat.

2. Add the garlic and cook for 1 minute.

3. Stir in the mushrooms and onion and cook for 6 to 8 minutes, until tender.

4. Add the vegetable broth and bring to a boil. Reduce heat and simmer for 20 minutes.

5. Stir in the spinach leaves, salt, and pepper.

6. Cook for 2 to 3 minutes, until the spinach is wilted. Serve hot.

Curried Lentil Soup

SERVES 6

Lentils are loaded with protein and dietary fiber, which will help keep you full while providing a number of other health benefits. Eating lentils has been shown to help reduce blood cholesterol and the risk for heart disease.

1 POUND DRY LENTILS

2 TABLESPOONS EXTRA-VIRGIN OLIVE OIL

1 TEASPOON MINCED GARLIC

1 YELLOW ONION, CHOPPED

1 LARGE STALK CELERY, CHOPPED

1 CUP CHOPPED TOMATOES

8 CUPS LOW-SODIUM VEGETABLE BROTH

½ TEASPOON GROUND CUMIN

1 TEASPOON SALT

¼ TEASPOON FRESHLY GROUND BLACK PEPPER

1. Rinse the lentils in fresh water and then drain and set aside.

2. In a stockpot, heat the olive oil over medium heat.

3. Add the garlic and cook for 1 minute.

4. Stir in the onion and celery and cook until tender, about 6 to 8 minutes.

5. Add the lentils, tomatoes, vegetable broth, ground cumin, salt, and pepper and bring the soup to a boil.

6. Reduce heat and simmer the soup, covered, for 35 to 40 minutes.

7. Remove the soup from heat and puree using an immersion blender. Serve hot.

Asian Vegetable Soup

If you are tired of boring vegetable soups, try out this Asian vegetable soup. Full of Eastern-influenced flavor and loaded with tender vegetables, this soup is sure to hit the spot.

2 TABLESPOONS EXTRA-VIRGIN OLIVE OIL

1 TEASPOON MINCED GARLIC

1 TABLESPOON GRATED GINGERROOT

2 PORTOBELLO MUSHROOM CAPS, SLICED

1 CUP CHOPPED CARROTS

1 CUP BEAN SPROUTS

1 CUP CHOPPED BOK CHOY

1 (8-OUNCE) CAN BAMBOO SHOOTS, DRAINED

6 CUPS LOW-SODIUM VEGETABLE BROTH

3 TABLESPOONS REDUCED-SODIUM SOY SAUCE

1 TEASPOON SESAME OIL

¼ CUP CHOPPED GREEN ONION

1. In a stockpot, heat the oil over medium heat.

2. Stir in the garlic and ginger and cook for 2 minutes, until fragrant.

3. Add the mushrooms, carrots, bean sprouts, bok choy, and bamboo shoots. Cook for about 3 minutes, stirring often.

4. Stir in the vegetable broth, soy sauce, and sesame oil and bring to a boil. Reduce heat and simmer for 20 minutes, until the vegetables are tender.

5. Serve the soup hot, garnished with the sliced green onion.

Creamy Cauliflower Soup

SERVES 4

This vegan "cream" of cauliflower soup is a cool and refreshing recipe, perfect for summer evenings.

2 TABLESPOONS COCONUT OIL

1 TEASPOON MINCED GARLIC

1 SMALL ONION, CHOPPED

1 LARGE STALK CELERY, CHOPPED

½ TEASPOON SALT

¼ TEASPOON FRESHLY GROUND BLACK PEPPER

4 CUPS LOW-SODIUM VEGETABLE BROTH

1 HEAD CAULIFLOWER, CHOPPED

1. In a large saucepan, heat the coconut oil over medium heat.

2. Stir in the garlic and cook for 1 minute.

3. Add the onion and celery and cook for 6 to 8 minutes, until softened.

4. Stir in the salt, pepper, and vegetable broth.

5. Add the cauliflower and then bring the soup to a boil.

6. Reduce heat and simmer for 20 to 25 minutes, until the cauliflower is tender.

7. Remove from heat and puree using an immersion blender.

8. Cool the soup to room temperature and then cover and chill for 2 to 4 hours. Serve cold.

Tomato Gazpacho

Gazpacho is a summer classic—loaded with fresh vegetables and served cold, this soup is just what you need to cool you down on a hot day.

6 RIPE ROMA TOMATOES, HALVED

1 SWEET RED PEPPER, SEEDED AND CHOPPED

1 GREEN BELL PEPPER, SEEDED AND CHOPPED

1 SMALL RED ONION, QUARTERED

1 CLOVE GARLIC, PEELED AND SLICED

3 CUPS TOMATO JUICE

¼ CUP WHITE WINE VINEGAR

¼ CUP EXTRA-VIRGIN OLIVE OIL

½ TEASPOON SALT

¼ TEASPOON FRESHLY GROUND BLACK PEPPER

1. Place the tomatoes in a food processor and pulse until finely chopped but not pureed. Transfer the tomatoes to a bowl.

2. Place the red and green peppers in a food processor and pulse until finely chopped. Transfer the peppers to the bowl with the tomatoes.

3. Place the onion and garlic in the food processor. Pulse until finely chopped and add to the bowl with the vegetables.

4. Stir in the tomato juice, vinegar, olive oil, salt, and pepper.

5. Cover the bowl and chill overnight. Serve cold.

Chilled Watermelon Soup

A unique twist on classic tomato gazpacho, this chilled watermelon soup is almost like having dessert for dinner.

6 CUPS CHOPPED WATERMELON

2 LARGE SEEDLESS CUCUMBERS, DICED

2 GREEN ONIONS, CHOPPED

½ CUP RICE WINE VINEGAR

¼ CUP FRESH CHOPPED CILANTRO LEAVES

1 TABLESPOON EXTRA-VIRGIN OLIVE OIL

3 TABLESPOONS CHOPPED FRESH MINT LEAVES

1. In a large bowl, combine all of the ingredients. Stir well and then cover and chill for 2 hours.

2. Mash the chopped watermelon using the back of a wooden spoon. Serve cold.

Cold "Cream"
of Asparagus Soup

SERVES 4 TO 6

You may be familiar with cream of asparagus soup, but cold "cream" of asparagus soup is a new experience altogether. There is just something about the way the flavors of fresh asparagus, garlic, and leeks combine when chilled that cannot be rivaled by a hot soup.

2 POUNDS FRESH ASPARAGUS SPEARS

8 CUPS WATER

3 TABLESPOONS EXTRA-VIRGIN OLIVE OIL

3 TABLESPOONS RICE FLOUR

1 YELLOW ONION, DICED

1 TEASPOON MINCED GARLIC

1 CUP CHOPPED LEEKS (WHITE AND LIGHT GREEN PARTS ONLY)

SALT TO TASTE

FRESHLY GROUND BLACK PEPPER TO TASTE

CILANTRO OR PARSLEY FOR GARNISHING (OPTIONAL)

1. Rinse the asparagus spears in cool water and then trim off the ends. Chop into 1/2-inch chunks.

2. In a large stockpot, bring the water to a boil and add the chopped asparagus. Boil for 3 minutes and then drain, reserving the liquid.

3. In a large saucepan, heat the olive oil over medium-high heat.

4. Whisk in the flour to form a roux (thickener) and then stir in the onion, garlic, and leeks.

5. Cook the mixture, stirring often, for 5 minutes, until the onions begin to soften.

6. Stir in the chopped asparagus and the reserved cooking liquid.

7. Bring the mixture to a simmer. Simmer, covered, for about 25 minutes, until the asparagus is tender.

8. Remove the soup from the heat and puree with an immersion blender.

9. Strain the soup through a mesh sieve and discard any solids.

10. Pour the soup into a large bowl and whisk in the salt and pepper.

11. Cover the soup and chill for 4 to 6 hours.

12. Garnish each serving with a sprig of fresh parsley or cilantro.

Creamy Cold Avocado Soup

SERVES 6

Avocado is an excellent source of heart-healthy monounsaturated fats. In this recipe, however, the health benefits of avocado play second fiddle to its fresh flavor and creamy texture.

3 RIPE AVOCADOS, PITTED, PEELED, AND CHOPPED

2 CUPS VEGETABLE BROTH

½ CUP MINCED RED ONION

¼ CUP FRESH CHOPPED CILANTRO LEAVES, PLUS EXTRA
    FOR GARNISHING

2 TABLESPOONS FRESH LEMON JUICE

1 TEASPOON SALT

1 CUP UNSWEETENED COCONUT MILK

1. In a food processor, combine the avocado, vegetable broth, red onion, cilantro, lemon juice, and salt. Blend the mixture until smooth and then pour into a serving bowl.

2. Cover and chill for several hours, until cold throughout.

3. Whisk in the coconut milk just before serving and garnish with cilantro leaves.

Sweet Potato Carrot Stew

SERVES 6

Sweet potatoes are valued for their detoxification benefits, and they have also been shown to support healthy digestion. This recipe combines the nutritional power of both sweet potatoes and carrots to form one delicious stew.

2 TABLESPOONS COCONUT OIL

1 TEASPOON MINCED GARLIC

1 YELLOW ONION, QUARTERED

2 LARGE CARROTS, CHOPPED

2 LARGE STALKS CELERY, CHOPPED

2 POUNDS SWEET POTATOES, PEELED AND ROUGHLY CHOPPED

2 CUPS LOW-SODIUM VEGETABLE BROTH

1½ TEASPOONS DRIED OREGANO

1 TEASPOON SALT

½ TEASPOON FRESHLY GROUND BLACK PEPPER

1. In a heavy skillet, heat the oil over medium-high heat.

2. Add the garlic and cook for 1 minute.

3. Stir in the onion, carrots, and celery and cook for 4 minutes.

4. Stir in the sweet potato and cook for 5 minutes.

5. Transfer the vegetables to a slow cooker.

6. In a medium bowl, whisk together the remaining ingredients, and then pour the mixture over the ingredients in the slow cooker.

7. Cover the slow cooker and cook on low heat for 4 to 6 hours. Serve hot.

Chickpea Butternut Squash Stew

SERVES 4

Chickpeas have a nutty flavor and buttery texture that blend perfectly with tender butternut squash in this hot and hearty stew.

1 MEDIUM BUTTERNUT SQUASH
2 TABLESPOONS COCONUT OIL
1 TEASPOON MINCED GARLIC
1 YELLOW ONION, CHOPPED
1 (15-OUNCE) CAN CHICKPEAS, RINSED AND DRAINED
1 (14-OUNCE) CAN CRUSHED TOMATOES
3 CUPS LOW-SODIUM VEGETABLE BROTH
½ CUP GOLDEN RAISINS
SALT TO TASTE
FRESHLY GROUND BLACK PEPPER TO TASTE

1. With a sharp knife, cut the butternut squash in half. Peel the squash and scoop out the seeds. Then chop into 1-inch cubes.

2. In a Dutch oven, heat the oil over medium-high heat.

3. Add the garlic and cook for 1 minute.

4. Stir in the onion and cook for 5 to 7 minutes, until softened.

5. Stir in the chickpeas, tomatoes, and vegetable broth.

6. Bring the stew to a boil and then reduce heat to low.

7. Stir in the raisins, salt, and pepper and simmer for 1 to 2 hours, until the squash is tender. Serve hot.

Garlic Red Bean Stew

Red kidney beans contain a variety of vitamins as well as calcium, iron, and folic acid. Beans are also an excellent source of dietary fiber, protein, and omega-3 fatty acids.

2 CUPS DRIED RED KIDNEY BEANS, RINSED WELL

8 CUPS WATER

¼ CUP EXTRA-VIRGIN OLIVE OIL

1 TABLESPOON MINCED GARLIC

1 LARGE ONION, CHOPPED

2 LARGE CARROTS, CHOPPED

1 SMALL ZUCCHINI, DICED

1 TEASPOON CHILI POWDER

½ TEASPOON SALT

1. In a stockpot, bring the beans and water to a boil. Reduce the heat to low and simmer, covered, for about 45 to 55 minutes, until the beans are tender.

2. Remove the stockpot from heat.

3. In a Dutch oven, heat the olive oil over medium-high heat.

4. Add the garlic and cook for 1 minute.

5. Stir in the onion and carrots and cook for 5 to 8 minutes.

6. Stir in cooked beans and remaining ingredients and simmer for 10 to 12 minutes. Serve hot.

Curried Vegetable Stew

SERVES 4 TO 6

This hearty vegetable stew is perfect for cold winter nights. Packed with tender vegetables and flavored with curry, this stew is sure to hit the spot.

2 TABLESPOON EXTRA-VIRGIN OLIVE OIL

1 TABLESPOON MINCED GARLIC

2 TABLESPOONS CURRY POWDER

¼ TEASPOON CAYENNE PEPPER

1 CUP CHOPPED CARROTS

1 CUP CHOPPED CELERY

1 CUP CHOPPED GREEN PEPPER

1 CUP CHOPPED ONION

1 POUND NEW POTATOES, QUARTERED

2 CUPS CHOPPED TOMATOES

½ CUP LOW-SODIUM VEGETABLE BROTH

1 CUP BABY SPINACH

1. In a heavy skillet, heat the olive oil over medium-high heat.

2. Add the garlic, curry powder, and cayenne and cook for 1 minute.

3. Stir in the carrots, celery, green pepper, and onion and cook for 5 minutes, until the onions become slightly tender.

4. Add the potatoes and cook for 3 minutes.

5. Stir in the chopped tomatoes and vegetable broth and bring to a simmer.

6. Simmer the soup, covered, for about 45 minutes.

7. Stir in the spinach leaves and simmer for 5 to 10 minutes, until the spinach is wilted.

8. Let the stew sit for 5 minutes and then serve hot.

CHAPTER THIRTEEN

Main Dishes

The dishes you will find in this chapter are anything but ordinary. Full of bold flavors like garlic, lemon, and rosemary, these entrées are sure to please. Feel free to eat these sumptuous dishes any time of day.

RECIPES INCLUDED IN THIS SECTION:

Quick and Easy Veggie Wrap

Rosemary Roasted Vegetables

Stuffed Zucchini Boats

Fried Zucchini Fritters

Crispy Corn Fritters

Baked Broccoli Casserole

Spicy Spaghetti Squash
     with Veggies

Lentil Sloppy Joes

Cilantro Quinoa Burgers

Vegan Chili

Black Bean Vegetable Enchiladas

Black Bean Avocado Tacos

Caramelized Onion
     Barbecue Quesadillas

Refried Bean Burritos

Stuffed Shells

Penne with Mushrooms
     and Artichokes

Garlic Red Pepper Pasta

No-Bake Spinach Mushroom
     Lasagna Casserole

Lemon-Garlic Squash and Linguine

Eggplant "Parmesan"

Carrot Leek Risotto

Ratatouille

Mediterranean-Style Pasta Salad

Couscous-Stuffed Baked Tomatoes

Vegetable Fried Rice

Vegetable Lo Mein

Quick and Easy Veggie Wrap

SERVES 1

This easy-to-make veggie wrap takes no more than a minute or two to throw together. It is the ideal on-the-go lunch and it is simple to eat at the office or even in the car.

1 LARGE VEGAN TORTILLA
1 TABLESPOON FRESH HUMMUS
3 OR 4 ROMAINE LETTUCE LEAVES
1 SMALL CARROT
1 GREEN ONION
¼ GREEN BELL PEPPER, HALVED AND SEEDED
¼ RED BELL PEPPER, HALVED AND SEEDED

1. Lay the tortilla flat on a plate and spread the hummus evenly over it.

2. Tear the lettuce leaves by hand and arrange them down center of the wrap.

3. Grate the carrot and chop the green onion and sprinkle both over the lettuce leaves.

4. Slice the peppers thin and add them to the wrap.

5. Fold up the bottom of the wrap to contain the ingredients and then roll it up and enjoy.

Rosemary Roasted Vegetables

These vegetables are incredibly easy to prepare but they taste anything but ordinary. Feel free to customize this recipe using fresh herbs from your garden or by adding your favorite dried herbs and spices.

2 CUPS CHOPPED SWEET POTATO

2 CUPS CHOPPED BROCCOLI FLORETS

2 CUPS CHOPPED CAULIFLOWER

1 LARGE YELLOW ONION, QUARTERED

1 CUP BUTTON MUSHROOMS

2 TABLESPOONS EXTRA-VIRGIN OLIVE OIL

SALT TO TASTE

FRESHLY GROUND BLACK PEPPER TO TASTE

¼ CUP VEGETABLE BROTH

2 TABLESPOONS DRIED ROSEMARY

1 TEASPOON DRIED OREGANO

1. Preheat oven to 400°F.

2. In a large bowl, combine the sweet potato, broccoli, cauliflower, onion, and mushrooms.

3. Toss with the olive oil and season with salt and pepper.

4. Transfer the vegetables to a glass baking dish.

5. In a small bowl, whisk together the remaining ingredients and pour over the vegetables.

6. Roast for 35 to 45 minutes, turning the vegetables halfway through.

Stuffed Zucchini Boats

SERVES 2

These stuffed zucchini boats are the perfect way to take advantage of summer farmers' markets. Feel free to add other fresh produce such as yellow squash, sweet corn, or fresh herbs.

2 MEDIUM ZUCCHINI
1 TO 2 TABLESPOONS EXTRA-VIRGIN OLIVE OIL
1 RIPE TOMATO, DICED
½ SMALL RED ONION, DICED
3 TABLESPOONS FRESH CHOPPED CILANTRO
3 TABLESPOONS FRESH CHOPPED BASIL LEAVES
SALT TO TASTE
FRESHLY GROUND BLACK PEPPER TO TASTE
¼ CUP PLAIN VEGAN BREADCRUMBS

1. Preheat oven to 350°F.

2. Line a small baking sheet with parchment paper.

3. Cut the zucchini in half lengthwise.

4. Carefully scoop out the middle of each zucchini half, leaving a border about ¼-inch thick on the sides and bottom.

5. Chop the zucchini insides that you scooped out, and transfer to a bowl.

6. Brush the zucchini boats lightly with olive oil, then place cut-side down on the baking sheet.

7. Bake for 8 to 10 minutes, until tender.

8. Stir the tomato, onion, cilantro, basil, salt, and pepper into the chopped zucchini.

9. Spoon the mixture into the zucchini boats and sprinkle with breadcrumbs.

10. Bake for 5 to 7 minutes, until the filling is hot.

Fried Zucchini Fritters

SERVES 4 TO 6

Zucchini is an excellent source of vitamin C as well as a variety of minerals including iron, magnesium, copper, potassium, and manganese.

2 MEDIUM ZUCCHINI

1 TEASPOON SALT

2 GREEN ONIONS, CHOPPED

FRESHLY GROUND BLACK PEPPER TO TASTE

2 TABLESPOONS WARM WATER

½ TABLESPOON ENER-G EGG REPLACER

½ CUP ALMOND FLOUR

½ TEASPOON BAKING POWDER

¼ TEASPOON PAPRIKA

COOKING SPRAY

1. Grate the zucchini with a hand grater or food processor.

2. Transfer the grated zucchini to a bowl and toss with the salt.

3. Let the zucchini sit for 10 minutes.

4. Then spread it out on paper towels and press with a clean towel to remove as much moisture as possible.

5. Transfer the pressed zucchini to a mixing bowl and stir in the green onions and ground pepper.

6. In a small bowl, combine the warm water and egg replacer and let sit for 3 to 5 minutes.

7. In another small bowl, whisk together the almond flour, baking powder, and paprika and then stir into the zucchini mixture.

8. Stir the egg replacer into the mixture.

continued ▶

9. Liberally oil a heavy skillet and heat over medium-high heat.

10. Spoon the zucchini mixture into the skillet in heaping tablespoons.

11. Cook each fritter for 3 to 5 minutes on each side until golden brown.

12. Drain the fritters on paper towels.

13. Serve warm.

Crispy Corn Fritters

SERVES 4 TO 6

These corn fritters are a delightful blend of sweet corn flavor and crispy crunch. During the summer, you might want to try this recipe using fresh corn off the cob.

2 TABLESPOONS EXTRA-VIRGIN OLIVE OIL, DIVIDED

1 CUP THAWED FROZEN SWEET CORN

½ CUP WHOLE WHEAT FLOUR

¾ TEASPOON BAKING POWDER

⅛ TEASPOON SALT

½ CUP UNSWEETENED ALMOND MILK

1 TABLESPOON APPLE CIDER VINEGAR

3 TABLESPOONS FRESH CHOPPED CHIVES

FRESHLY GROUND BLACK PEPPER

1. Preheat oven to 350°F.

2. Line a baking sheet with foil.

3. In a heavy skillet, heat 1 tablespoon of oil and then add the corn. Cook the corn for 2 to 3 minutes, until heated through.

4. In a mixing bowl, whisk together the flour, baking powder, and salt.

5. Beat in the almond milk, cider vinegar, and chives, and stir in the cooked corn. Season with pepper to taste.

6. Add the remaining tablespoon of oil to the skillet and reheat over medium-high heat.

7. Spoon the corn mixture into the skillet by heaping tablespoons, leaving at least 1 inch between the fritters.

8. Cook for 2 to 3 minutes per side, until lightly browned.

9. Transfer the fritters to the baking sheet and bake for 5 to 10 minutes, until crisp.

10. Drain fritters on paper towels and serve hot.

Baked Broccoli Casserole

SERVES 6 TO 8

This baked broccoli casserole is a quick and easy meal ideal for a casual family dinner at home. You may be surprised to find that your kids love it so much they begin to request it.

2½ CUPS EGGLESS NOODLES

COOKING SPRAY

1¼ CUPS WATER

1 MEDIUM SWEET POTATO, PEELED AND CHOPPED

1 SMALL CARROT, PEELED AND DICED

¼ CUP DICED YELLOW ONION

1 TEASPOON MINCED GARLIC

¼ CUP EXTRA-VIRGIN OLIVE OIL

¼ CUP RAW CASHEW HALVES

1 TABLESPOON FRESH LEMON JUICE

SALT TO TASTE

FRESHLY GROUND BLACK PEPPER TO TASTE

2 CUPS CHOPPED BROCCOLI FLORETS

1. Preheat oven to 350°F.

2. Bring a pot of salted water to boil and add the noodles. Cook the noodles to al dente according to the directions on the box. Drain and set aside.

3. Oil a 2-quart baking dish.

4. In a medium saucepan, stir together the water, sweet potato, carrot, onion, and garlic.

5. Bring the mixture to a boil and then reduce heat. Simmer for 8 to 10 minutes, until the vegetables are tender.

6. Transfer the vegetables to a blender and add the olive oil, cashews, lemon juice, salt, pepper, and broccoli.

7. Blend the mixture until smooth and then stir into the cooked pasta.

8. Transfer the mixture to the prepared baking dish and bake for 25 to 30 minutes, until hot and bubbling.

Spicy Spaghetti Squash with Veggies

SERVES 6

Spaghetti squash is a small dish that goes a long way. It is also incredibly versatile in terms of preparation. Simply bake the squash and serve it sautéed with your favorite vegetables, or use it as a pasta alternative.

1 LARGE SPAGHETTI SQUASH
COOKING SPRAY
2 TABLESPOONS EXTRA-VIRGIN OLIVE OIL
1 JALAPEÑO, SEEDED AND MINCED
1 TEASPOON GRATED GINGERROOT
1 TEASPOON MINCED GARLIC
1 YELLOW ONION, CHOPPED
1 GREEN BELL PEPPER, SEEDED AND CHOPPED
1 RED BELL PEPPER, SEEDED AND CHOPPED
1 CUP DICED TOMATOES
SALT TO TASTE
CAYENNE PEPPER TO TASTE

1. Preheat oven to 350°F.

2. Cut the spaghetti squash in half and scoop out the seeds.

3. Place the squash halves cut-side down in a lightly greased glass baking dish.

4. Bake the squash for 30 minutes or until a sharp knife inserted into the skin of the squash slides in easily.

5. Remove the dish from the oven and set aside until the squash is cool enough to handle.

6. Meanwhile, heat the oil in a heavy skillet.

7. Stir in the jalapeño, gingerroot, and garlic. Cook for 1 minute.

8. Add the onion and bell peppers and cook for 4 to 6 minutes, until tender.

9. Stir in the diced tomatoes and cook for 2 minutes longer.

10. Shred the cooked squash with a fork and add it to the skillet with the vegetables.

11. Season with salt and cayenne pepper to taste and cook until heated through.

Lentil Sloppy Joes

Sloppy Joes are a family favorite and these are irresistible. Meatless doesn't necessarily mean flavorless, and these Sloppy Joes are the proof.

1 TABLESPOON EXTRA-VIRGIN OLIVE OIL
1 TEASPOON MINCED GARLIC
2 TEASPOONS CHILI POWDER
1 ONION, DICED
1 RED BELL PEPPER, SEEDED AND DICED
1 (15-OUNCE) CAN LENTILS, RINSED AND DRAINED
1½ CUPS WATER
½ CUP KETCHUP
1 TABLESPOON LOW-SODIUM SOY SAUCE

1. In a saucepan, heat the oil over medium heat. Stir in the garlic and chili powder and cook for about 1 minute.

2. Add the onion and red pepper and cook for 5 to 7 minutes, until tender.

3. Stir in the remaining ingredients and bring the mixture to a boil.

4. Reduce the heat and simmer the mixture for 15 to 20 minutes, until thick and bubbling.

5. Serve the mixture hot on fresh sandwich rolls.

. . . .

Ease your way into a vegan or vegetarian diet by making meat-free versions of your favorite meals. Substitute the beef in tacos or burritos with beans and grilled veggies or try topping homemade pizza with soy cheese and chopped vegetables.

. . . .

Cilantro Quinoa Burgers

Quinoa is often referred to as a "super food" because it has such a high nutrient content. In addition to being a good source of vegetarian protein, quinoa is also rich in dietary fiber and other essential vitamins and minerals.

¼ CUP DRY QUINOA

½ CUP WATER

PINCH OF SALT

1 (15-OUNCE) CAN BLACK BEANS, RINSED AND DRAINED

½ CUP PLAIN VEGAN BREADCRUMBS

¼ CUP FRESH CHOPPED CILANTRO LEAVES

2 TABLESPOONS MINCED RED ONION

SALT TO TASTE

FRESHLY GROUND BLACK PEPPER TO TASTE

2 TABLESPOONS EXTRA-VIRGIN OLIVE OIL

1. In a small saucepan, stir together the quinoa, water, and salt.

2. Bring the mixture to a boil and then reduce the heat and simmer for 15 minutes, until the quinoa absorbs all the water. Set the quinoa aside, covered.

3. Place the black beans in a bowl and mash gently with a fork.

4. Stir in the remaining ingredients, including the cooked quinoa but not the olive oil, until well combined.

5. Shape the mixture into 5 patties.

6. Heat the oil in a heavy skillet and add the quinoa patties.

7. Cook for 2 to 3 minutes on each side until heated through.

8. Serve hot.

Vegan Chili

SERVES 6 TO 8

This vegetarian chili is hot and hearty—the ultimate meal for a cold night or for when you just need a filling meal.

2 TABLESPOONS EXTRA-VIRGIN OLIVE OIL

1 TABLESPOON MINCED GARLIC

3 TABLESPOONS CHILI POWDER

¾ TEASPOON DRIED OREGANO

½ TEASPOON SALT

PINCH OF CAYENNE (OPTIONAL)

1 RED ONION, DICED

1 RED BELL PEPPER, DICED

1 YELLOW SQUASH, CHOPPED

1 (14.5-OUNCE) CAN ITALIAN STEWED TOMATOES

1 (15-OUNCE) CAN BLACK BEANS, RINSED AND DRAINED

1 CUP THAWED FROZEN CORN

1. In a Dutch oven, heat the olive over medium heat.

2. Stir in the garlic, chili powder, oregano, salt, and cayenne and cook for 1 minute, until fragrant.

3. Add the onion and red pepper and cook until tender, about 5 minutes.

4. Stir in the yellow squash and stewed tomatoes and simmer for about 15 minutes, until the vegetables are tender.

5. Add the black beans and corn and stir well to incorporate.

6. Simmer for 5 minutes until heated through.

7. Serve hot.

Black Bean Vegetable Enchiladas

SERVES 6

These vegetable enchiladas are full of authentic Mexican flavor and tender black beans. Use the Enchilada Sauce recipe from Chapter 10 to make this dish completely homemade.

½ TABLESPOON EXTRA-VIRGIN OLIVE OIL

1 CLOVE GARLIC, MINCED

1 YELLOW ONION, CHOPPED

1 GREEN BELL PEPPER, SEEDED AND CHOPPED

1 RED BELL PEPPER, SEEDED AND CHOPPED

1 (15-OUNCE) CAN BLACK BEANS, RINSED AND DRAINED

½ CUP THAWED FROZEN CORN

2 TABLESPOONS TACO SEASONING

6 LARGE WHOLE WHEAT TORTILLAS, WARMED

½ CUP ENCHILADA SAUCE

1. Heat the oil in a heavy skillet over medium heat. Add the garlic and cook for 1 minute.

2. Stir in the onion and bell peppers. Cook, stirring, for 5 to 7 minutes.

3. Stir in the black beans, corn, and taco seasoning.

4. Cook the mixture for 2 to 3 minutes, until heated through.

5. Spoon about ½ cup of the black bean vegetable mixture down the center of each whole wheat tortilla.

6. Roll the tortillas up around the filling and place in a greased baking dish.

7. After placing all the tortillas in the dish, top with enchilada sauce.

8. Bake the enchiladas for 25 to 30 minutes, until hot and bubbling.

Black Bean Avocado Tacos

SERVES 4

These tacos are a unique blend of flavors and textures. From the cool, creamy taste of fresh avocado to the refreshing taste of cilantro, these tacos are sure to wake up your taste buds.

2 RIPE AVOCADOS, PITTED AND PEELED
1 TEASPOON MINCED GARLIC
½ TEASPOON GROUND CUMIN
2 TABLESPOONS FRESH LIME JUICE
8 WHITE CORN TORTILLAS, WARMED
1 CUP COOKED BLACK BEANS
1 CUP SHREDDED LETTUCE
½ CUP DICED TOMATO
¼ CUP FRESH CHOPPED CILANTRO LEAVES
½ JALAPEÑO PEPPER, SEEDED AND MINCED

1. Place the avocado in a bowl and mash gently with the back of a fork.

2. Using the fork, stir in the garlic, cumin, and lime juice.

3. Spoon the avocado mixture down the center of the warmed tortillas and top with cooked black beans.

4. Combine the remaining ingredients in a bowl and toss well to combine.

5. Top each taco with some of the lettuce-tomato mixture. Fold the tortilla over the mixture and serve.

Caramelized Onion Barbecue Quesadillas

SERVES 1

These quesadillas are the perfect way to make use of your own homemade Sweet Barbecue Sauce in Chapter 10.

1½ TABLESPOONS EXTRA-VIRGIN OLIVE OIL
1 CLOVE GARLIC, MINCED
1 SMALL ONION, SLICED THIN
1½ TABLESPOONS VEGAN BARBECUE SAUCE
1 (8-INCH) WHOLE WHEAT TORTILLA
COOKING SPRAY

1. In a small skillet, heat the olive oil over medium heat. Add the garlic and cook for 1 minute.

2. Stir in the onions and toss to coat with oil.

3. Reduce the heat to medium-low and cook the onions until caramelized, about 12 to 15 minutes.

4. Spoon the barbecue sauce onto the tortilla and spread evenly.

5. Spoon the onion and garlic mixture onto half of the tortilla and fold the empty half over top.

6. Lightly spray the top of the quesadilla with cooking spray and place it in the skillet, flipping it so the sprayed side is down.

7. Cook for 2 minutes, until the tortilla is browned.

8. Spray the top of the tortilla with cooking spray and carefully flip and cook until browned on the other side.

9. Cut into 2 pieces to serve.

Refried Bean Burritos

SERVES 4

Refried bean burritos are an excellent option for a quick meal. You can use the Refried Beans recipe in Chapter 11, or use the canned variety.

8 YELLOW CORN TORTILLAS
2 CUPS REFRIED BEANS
1½ CUPS COOKED MEXICAN RICE
FRESH SALSA AND/OR GUACAMOLE

1. Wrap the tortillas in a paper towel, two at a time, and microwave on high heat for 5 to 8 seconds, until warmed.

2. Spoon about ¼ cup refried beans down the center of each tortilla.

3. Top the beans with about 2 tablespoons of Mexican rice.

4. Roll the tortillas up around the filling and serve with salsa and/or guacamole.

Stuffed Shells

SERVES 4 TO 5

By substituting extra-firm tofu for the ricotta traditionally used in stuffed shells, you can make your own vegan version that will fool them all. Feel free to add more fresh herbs, if you like, or omit the spinach.

COOKING SPRAY

1 (12-OUNCE) BOX JUMBO PASTA SHELLS

1 (14-OUNCE) BOX EXTRA-FIRM TOFU

½ TABLESPOON EXTRA-VIRGIN OLIVE OIL

2 TEASPOONS MINCED GARLIC

1 MEDIUM VIDALIA ONION, DICED

1 CUP FRESH CHOPPED BABY SPINACH

½ CUP FRESH CHOPPED BASIL LEAVES

3 TABLESPOONS NUTRITIONAL YEAST

1 TABLESPOON FRESH LEMON JUICE

SALT TO TASTE

FRESHLY GROUND BLACK PEPPER TO TASTE

3 CUPS VEGAN PASTA SAUCE

1. Preheat oven to 350°F.

2. Lightly oil a 9 × 13-inch glass baking dish.

3. Bring a large pot of water to boil and add the shells.

4. Cook the pasta to al dente according to the directions, and then drain and set aside.

5. Remove the tofu from the box and rinse in cool water. Wrap the tofu block in several layers of paper towels and place a heavy book on top of it. Press the tofu to extract the excess water, applying pressure as evenly as possible.

6. Transfer the pressed tofu to a food processor and blend until smooth.

continued ▶

7. In a skillet, heat the oil over medium heat. Add the garlic and onion.

8. Cook the garlic and onion for about 5 minutes, until softened.

9. Stir in the spinach and basil and cook for another 2 to 3 minutes.

10. Spoon the blended tofu into the skillet and whisk in the nutritional yeast, lemon juice, salt, and pepper.

11. Cook the mixture for 8 to 10 minutes, until most of the liquid has cooked off.

12. Spoon 1 cup of pasta sauce into the prepared baking dish and spread evenly.

13. Spoon 1½ to 2 tablespoons of the tofu mixture into each cooked shell and arrange the shells in the baking dish.

14. Pour the rest of the pasta sauce over the shells and cover the dish with foil.

15. Poke several holes in the foil to vent steam and then bake for 20 minutes, until heated through.

16. Let the shells sit for 10 minutes, covered, before serving.

. . . .

Did you know that obesity is one of the most serious health problems in the United States and other Western cultures, but it is also one of the most preventable? Switching to a plant-based diet provides relief from a number of serious health problems and can also help you to reduce your calorie intake and maintain a healthy body weight.

. . . .

Penne with Mushrooms and Artichokes

SERVES 4 TO 6

This dish is full of unique flavor, accented with tender mushrooms and artichokes. If you are looking for a meal that is out of the ordinary, try this penne with mushrooms and artichokes.

3 TABLESPOONS EXTRA-VIRGIN OLIVE OIL, DIVIDED

1 TEASPOON MINCED GARLIC

2 CUPS SLICED MUSHROOMS

¾ CUP VEGAN WHITE WINE, DIVIDED

SALT TO TASTE

FRESHLY GROUND BLACK PEPPER TO TASTE

½ CUP CHOPPED YELLOW ONION

1 (14-OUNCE) CAN ARTICHOKES, DRAINED AND SLICED

2 TABLESPOONS FRESH CHOPPED THYME

1 (16-OUNCE) BOX PENNE PASTA, COOKED

PARSLEY, FOR GARNISHING

1. In a heavy skillet, heat 1½ tablespoons of the oil over medium heat.

2. Add the garlic and cook for 1 minute.

3. Stir in the mushrooms until coated with oil.

4. Stir in ¼ cup white wine and cook until most of the liquid has evaporated.

5. Remove from the heat and season with salt and pepper to taste.

6. Heat the remaining oil in another skillet over medium heat.

7. Stir in the onion and cook for 3 to 5 minutes.

8. Add the sliced artichoke and stir well.

continued ▶

9. Stir in the rest of the wine and fresh thyme and cook until most of the liquid has been absorbed.

10. Spoon the mushroom and artichoke mixtures into a serving bowl.

11. Drain the pasta when cooked and add to the bowl with the mushroom and artichoke mixture.

12. Toss to combine.

13. Serve garnished with fresh parsley.

Garlic Red Pepper Pasta

Red peppers are a good source of vitamin C, which helps support healing as well as gum and teeth health. As simple as it may be, this recipe is full of flavor.

1½ TABLESPOONS EXTRA-VIRGIN OLIVE OIL

1 TABLESPOON MINCED GARLIC

2 SWEET RED PEPPERS, SEEDED AND SLICED THIN

1 (16-OUNCE) BOX FARFALLE PASTA, COOKED

½ BUNCH PARSLEY, FINELY CHOPPED

SALT TO TASTE

FRESHLY GROUND BLACK PEPPER TO TASTE

1. In a large skillet, heat the oil over medium heat.

2. Add the garlic and cook for 1 minute.

3. Stir in the red peppers and cook for 5 to 6 minutes, until tender.

4. Add the cooked pasta and parsley and toss to combine.

5. Season the pasta with salt and pepper to taste and cook until heated through.

6. Serve hot.

No-Bake Spinach Mushroom Lasagna Casserole

If you like the flavor of lasagna but don't want to put all the time and effort into making it, this no-bake casserole is an excellent alternative.

4 OUNCES FRESH FIRM TOFU

1 CUP PASTA SAUCE

2 TABLESPOONS EXTRA-VIRGIN OLIVE OIL

2 TEASPOONS MINCED GARLIC

½ TEASPOON DRIED OREGANO

¼ TEASPOON DRIED THYME

1 POUND SLICED MUSHROOMS

10 OUNCES FRESH BABY SPINACH

1 (16-OUNCE) BOX ROTINI PASTA, COOKED

SALT TO TASTE

FRESHLY GROUND BLACK PEPPER TO TASTE

1. Place the tofu and pasta sauce in a food processor and blend until smooth.

2. In a large skillet, heat the olive oil over medium heat. Add the garlic, oregano, and thyme. Cook for 1 minute.

3. Stir in the mushrooms and cook until the liquid begins to evaporate.

4. Add the spinach and cook for about 2 minutes until wilted.

5. Stir in the blended tofu along with the cooked pasta.

6. Season with salt and pepper and serve when heated through.

Lemon-Garlic Squash and Linguine

SERVES 6 TO 8

This linguine is a simple way to get that "eating out" feeling at home. Surprisingly easy to prepare, this recipe is full of flavor and sure to make you feel as if you are dining in a fine restaurant.

2 TABLESPOONS OLIVE OIL
2 TABLESPOONS MINCED GARLIC
1 MEDIUM YELLOW SQUASH, SLICED THIN
¼ CUP FRESH LEMON JUICE
1 TEASPOON CORNSTARCH
1 (16-OUNCE) BOX LINGUINE, COOKED
SALT TO TASTE
FRESHLY GROUND BLACK PEPPER TO TASTE

1. In a large skillet, heat the oil over medium heat. Add the garlic and cook for 1 minute.

2. Stir in the squash and cook for 3 to 4 minutes, until tender.

3. In a small bowl, whisk together the lemon juice and cornstarch.

4. Then stir the mixture into the skillet and cook for 1 minute, until it begins to thicken.

5. Add the cooked pasta and toss to coat.

6. Season with salt and pepper and then cook until heated through.

7. Serve hot.

Eggplant "Parmesan"

SERVES 4

This eggplant recipe doesn't actually contain parmesan cheese, but it is inspired by the traditional Italian-style recipe. Quick and easy to make, this recipe may become one of your family's go-to meals.

1 POUND EGGPLANT

1 TEASPOON SALT

1 CUP UNSWEETENED COCONUT MILK

¾ CUP ALMOND FLOUR

1 TEASPOON DRIED OREGANO

1 TEASPOON DRIED THYME

2 CUPS PLAIN VEGAN BREADCRUMBS

1. Preheat oven to 450°F.

2. Line a baking sheet with parchment paper.

3. Peel the eggplant carefully with a sharp knife and cut it into ¼-inch slices.

4. Arrange the slices on paper towels and sprinkle with salt.

5. Let the eggplant sit for about 20 minutes. Then pat dry with paper towel or a clean cloth.

6. In a mixing bowl, whisk together the coconut milk, flour, oregano, and thyme and then pour into a shallow dish.

7. Dip the eggplant slices in the milk mixture and then coat with the breadcrumbs.

8. Spread out the breaded eggplant slices on the baking sheet and bake for 6 to 8 minutes per side until crisp and browned.

9. Serve the eggplant hot over a bed of pasta with pasta sauce.

Carrot Leek Risotto

SERVES 4 TO 6

This carrot leek risotto is like nothing you have ever tasted before. Thick and creamy, accented with the flavors of fresh carrot and leek, this risotto will certainly hit the spot.

6½ CUPS VEGETABLE BROTH

2 TABLESPOONS EXTRA-VIRGIN OLIVE OIL

1 POUND FRESH CARROTS, SLICED THIN

2 MEDIUM LEEKS, RINSED AND CHOPPED (WHITE AND LIGHT GREEN
    PARTS ONLY)

1½ CUPS ARBORIO RICE

1 TEASPOON MINCED GARLIC

SALT TO TASTE

FRESHLY GROUND BLACK PEPPER TO TASTE

½ CUP VEGAN WHITE WINE

2 TABLESPOONS FRESH CHOPPED PARSLEY

1 TABLESPOON FRESH CHOPPED CHIVES

1 TEASPOON FRESH LEMON JUICE

1. In a large saucepan, bring the vegetable broth to a simmer.

2. In a separate saucepan, heat the oil over medium heat. Stir in the carrots and leeks and cook for 3 to 4 minutes, until slightly tender.

3. Then, stir in the rice and garlic and season with salt and pepper.

4. Cook for several minutes, until the grains of rice begin to crackle and pop.

5. Whisk in the wine and cook until it has almost evaporated.

6. Spoon about ½ cup of the warmed vegetable broth from step 1 into the saucepan. Cook, stirring, until the liquid is almost absorbed.

continued ▶

7. Keep adding the broth, about ½ cup at a time, after the liquid has been absorbed.

8. Cook the rice for a total of about 20 to 25 minutes, until it is tender but not mushy.

9. Remove the pan from the heat once the rice is tender.

10. Stir in another ½ cup of broth along with the parsley, chives, and lemon juice.

11. Ladle into bowls and serve immediately.

Ratatouille

SERVES 6

This recipe is a delicious mixture of zucchini, squash, eggplant, and tomato, all garnished with a hint of garlic and fresh basil.

1 MEDIUM ZUCCHINI
1 MEDIUM YELLOW SUMMER SQUASH
1 POUND EGGPLANT
1 POUND RIPE RED TOMATOES
COOKING SPRAY
1 TABLESPOON MINCED GARLIC
2 TABLESPOONS FRESH CHOPPED BASIL LEAVES

1. Preheat oven to 250°F.

2. Slice the vegetables thick, about ½ inch for each slice.

3. Lightly oil a round casserole dish and arrange a layer of zucchini slices on the bottom.

4. Top with a layer of squash, then the eggplant and tomato.

5. Sprinkle the garlic and basil on top.

6. Bake, covered, for 1 to 1½ hours, until vegetables are tender.

7. Serve hot over a bed of fresh couscous.

Mediterranean-Style Pasta Salad

SERVES 6 TO 8

This pasta salad is full of Greek style, utilizing the flavors of olive oil, red wine vinegar, black olives, and even fresh basil.

1 (12- TO 16-OUNCE) BOX ROTINI PASTA
¼ CUP DICED RED ONION
¼ CUP DICED AND SEEDED GREEN PEPPER
¼ CUP FRESH CHOPPED BASIL LEAVES
2 TABLESPOONS EXTRA-VIRGIN OLIVE OIL
1 TABLESPOON RED WINE VINEGAR
¼ CUP SLICED BLACK OLIVES
1 TEASPOON DRIED OREGANO
PINCH OF SALT
PINCH OF FRESHLY GROUND BLACK PEPPER

1. Bring a large pot of water to boil and add the pasta.

2. Cook the pasta to al dente according to the directions and then drain.

3. Rinse the pasta in cool water, drain, and transfer it to a large bowl.

4. Stir in the red onion, green pepper, and basil leaves.

5. In another bowl, whisk together the remaining ingredients and add to the pasta.

6. Toss to coat, then chill until ready to serve.

Couscous-Stuffed Baked Tomatoes

You may be familiar with stuffed peppers, but these couscous-stuffed baked tomatoes might be new to you. On its own, couscous can seem a little plain— but baked inside a fresh tomato, it is nothing short of heavenly.

COOKING SPRAY

4 LARGE RIPE TOMATOES

¼ CUP VEGETABLE BROTH OR WATER

¼ CUP DRY COUSCOUS

PINCH OF SALT

2 TABLESPOONS EXTRA-VIRGIN OLIVE OIL

3 TABLESPOONS PLAIN BREADCRUMBS

2 TEASPOONS DRIED ITALIAN SEASONING

1 TEASPOON MINCED GARLIC

1. Preheat oven to 350°F.

2. Lightly oil a glass baking dish.

3. Slice the tops off the tomatoes and reserve them for later. Carefully scoop out the seeds.

3. Arrange the tomatoes cut-side down on paper towels to drain.

4. In a small saucepan, bring the vegetable broth or water to a boil and then remove from heat.

5. Immediately stir in the couscous and salt. Cover the saucepan and let the couscous sit for 10 minutes or until it has absorbed the liquid.

6. Place the couscous in a bowl and stir in the remaining ingredients.

continued ▶

7. Spoon the couscous mixture into the tomatoes and place the tomatoes in the prepared baking dish.

8. Place the tops on the tomatoes and bake for 20 to 30 minutes, until the tomatoes are tender and the filling heated through.

. . . .

Did you know that some of your favorite celebrities follow a vegan or vegetarian lifestyle? Some notable vegetarians include Bob Harper, Sir Paul McCartney, Casey Affleck, Natalie Portman, and Tobey Maguire. Even professional and Olympic athletes like Keith Holmes, Carl Lewis, and Ricky Williams follow a meat-free diet.

. . . .

Vegetable Fried Rice

SERVES 6

This vegetable fried rice is easy to prepare and a wonderful blend of whole grain brown rice and fresh vegetables. Whip up a big batch and then enjoy the leftovers all week long.

½ CUP TEXTURED VEGETABLE PROTEIN

½ CUP WATER

2½ TABLESPOONS SOY SAUCE, DIVIDED

3 TABLESPOONS EXTRA-VIRGIN OLIVE OIL

1 TEASPOON MINCED GARLIC

1 CUP CHOPPED YELLOW ONION

1 CUP CHOPPED CARROT

1 CUP CHOPPED MUSHROOMS

¼ CUP CHOPPED CELERY

3 CUPS COOKED BROWN RICE

¼ TEASPOON GROUND GINGERROOT

¼ TEASPOON FRESHLY GROUND BLACK PEPPER

1. In a mixing bowl, combine the textured vegetable protein, water, and 1 tablespoon of soy sauce. Stir well and set aside for about 5 minutes, until the liquid is absorbed.

2. In a heavy skillet, heat the oil over medium heat.

3. Add the garlic and cook for 1 minute.

4. Stir in the onion, carrot, mushroom, and celery.

5. Cook for 3 to 4 minutes, until the onions begin to soften.

6. Move the vegetables to the sides of the skillet and stir in the textured vegetable protein.

7. Add the remaining soy sauce and then stir in the cooked rice.

8. Stir in the ground gingerroot and pepper, stirring well to coat the rice with sauce.

9. Remove from the heat and set aside for 3 to 5 minutes before serving.

Vegetable Lo Mein

SERVES 4

If you are a fan of Asian cuisine, this vegetable lo mein is sure to please. Made with egg-free noodles and a medley of fresh vegetables, this is the ultimate ethnic vegan dish.

2 TABLESPOONS EXTRA-VIRGIN OLIVE OIL

1 TEASPOON MINCED GARLIC

1 TEASPOON FRESH GROUND GINGERROOT

4 CUPS FROZEN STIR-FRY VEGETABLES

3 TABLESPOONS LOW-SODIUM SOY SAUCE

2 TEASPOONS DARK SESAME OIL

8 OUNCES EGG-FREE SPAGHETTI, COOKED AL DENTE

SLICED GREEN ONION TO TASTE

1. In a large skillet, heat the oil over medium-high heat.

2. Add the garlic and ginger and cook for 1 minute.

3. Stir in the frozen vegetables and cook for about 5 minutes, until thawed and heated through.

4. In a small bowl, whisk together the soy sauce and sesame oil and then stir the mixture into the skillet.

5. Add the noodles and toss to coat.

6. Serve hot, garnished with sliced green onion.

CHAPTER FOURTEEN

Desserts and Snacks

Without using dairy products like milk and cream, you may find it hard to believe that you can still make delicious desserts. Vegan desserts are full of flavor, however, and come in a variety of forms. From traditional favorites including cupcakes and cookies to fruit pizza and raw fudge, you are sure to find a number of mouthwatering desserts in this chapter, as well as snacks worthy of any vegan lunch bag.

RECIPES INCLUDED IN THIS SECTION:

Cinnamon Baked Bananas

Sweet Cinnamon Applesauce

Brown Sugar Baked Apples

Tropical Fruit Salad

Sliced Fruit Pizza

Herb-Marinated Nectarines

Maple-Glazed Poached Pears

Balsamic Grilled Peaches

Fresh-Fruit Freeze Pops

Blueberry Sorbet

Raspberry Lime Sorbet

Raspberry "Ice Cream"

Whipped Coconut Cream

Whipped Chocolate Mousse

Strawberry Chocolate Trifle

Raw Coconut Fudge

Raw Cinnamon Raisin Cookies

Almond Shortbread Cookies

Sugared Chocolate Grahams

Lemon Vanilla Cupcakes

Gluten-Free Chocolate Cupcakes

Cinnamon Carrot Cake

Red Velvet Cake

Fruit and Nut Granola Bars

Cinnamon Raisin Oatmeal Bars

Chocolate Peanut Butter Bars

Chocolate Peanut Butter Rice Bars

Spiced Pumpkin Bars

Hot-and-Salty Mixed Nuts

Sweet-and-Salty Trail Mix

Baked Sweet Potato Chips

Sugared Apple Chips

Cinnamon Baked Apple Chips

Sesame Kale Chips

Cinnamon Baked Bananas

SERVES 2

If you are looking for a simple yet unique dessert recipe to satisfy even the pickiest of eaters, these cinnamon baked bananas are sure to do the trick.

2 MEDIUM BANANAS
1½ TABLESPOONS PURE MAPLE SYRUP
1 TO 2 TEASPOONS GROUND CINNAMON
PINCH OF NUTMEG

1. Preheat oven to 350°F.

2. Leaving the bananas in their peels, carefully slice the bananas lengthwise, leaving the bottom of the peels intact.

3. Set the bananas on a parchment-lined baking sheet.

4. Pull the peels apart and drizzle the bananas with maple syrup. Sprinkle with cinnamon and nutmeg.

5. Bake for 8 to 10 minutes, until hot and tender.

Sweet Cinnamon Applesauce

MAKES ABOUT 2 CUPS

If you've never made your own applesauce before, you may be surprised at how easy it is. Flavored with light brown sugar and a hint of cinnamon, this applesauce will go fast.

4 SWEET APPLES, PEELED AND CORED
1 TABLESPOON LIGHT BROWN SUGAR
PINCH OF GROUND CINNAMON OR NUTMEG

1. Coarsely chop the apples and place them in a microwave-safe bowl.

2. Cover the bowl with plastic wrap and microwave on high power for 1 minute.

3. Stir the apples and then microwave for 3 minutes more, until the apples are softened, stirring after each minute.

4. Spoon the mixture into a food processor and blend until smooth.

5. Add the brown sugar and cinnamon and pulse to combine.

6. Serve the applesauce warm or chill before serving.

Brown Sugar Baked Apples

SERVES 4

Baked apples are a quick and easy dessert that are sure to satisfy your sweet tooth. The best news of all is that this recipe is very easy to multiply, so you can make enough baked apples to go around.

4 RIPE GALA APPLES
1 CUP CHOPPED ALMONDS
1½ TABLESPOONS BROWN SUGAR
1½ TEASPOONS GROUND CINNAMON
1 CUP APPLE JUICE

1. Preheat oven to 350°F.

2. Use an apple corer to remove the core from the apples without punching through the bottom.

3. Carefully scoop out and retain as much of the apple pulp as you can without breaking through the sides of the apple.

4. Place the almonds in a food processor and pulse to finely chop.

5. Add the apple pulp, brown sugar, and cinnamon.

6. Pulse to blend and then spoon the filling into the apples.

7. Arrange the apples in a glass baking dish and pour the apple juice into the bottom of the dish.

8. Bake for 8 to 12 minutes, until the apples are tender.

Tropical Fruit Salad

SERVES 3 TO 4

Made with kiwi, pineapple, mango, banana, and orange, this fruit salad may just be a little bite of tropical heaven.

2 RIPE KIWIFRUIT, PEELED AND SLICED

1½ CUPS PINEAPPLE CHUNKS

1 RIPE MANGO, PEELED, PITTED, AND CHOPPED

1 RIPE BANANA, PEELED AND CHOPPED

1 NAVEL ORANGE, PEELED AND CHOPPED

1. Combine all of the chopped fruit in a serving bowl.

2. Toss well to combine and chill before serving, if desired.

Sliced Fruit Pizza

SERVES 6

If you are looking for a dessert that has style as well as flavor, this sliced fruit pizza may be just the thing. Use your creativity to arrange the fruit slices in whatever design you like to create a stunning and sweet dessert.

¼ CUP PLUS 1 TABLESPOON VEGAN SHORTENING

⅓ CUP UNBLEACHED ALL-PURPOSE FLOUR

PINCH OF SALT

3 TO 4 TABLESPOONS ICE WATER

6 TABLESPOONS VEGAN BUTTER SUBSTITUTE

1 CUP TOFU CREAM CHEESE

3½ TO 4 CUPS POWDERED SUGAR

1 TEASPOON ALMOND EXTRACT

1 RIPE PEACH, PITTED AND SLICED THIN

1 RIPE KIWIFRUIT, PEELED AND SLICED THIN

½ CUP FRESH SLICED STRAWBERRIES

½ CUP FRESH BLACKBERRIES

¼ CUP FRESH BLUEBERRIES

MAPLE SYRUP (OPTIONAL)

1. Preheat oven to 375°F.

2. Place the shortening in a mixing bowl and beat by hand until smooth.

3. Beat in the flour and salt until well combined.

4. Add the ice water 1 tablespoon at a time, beating for 10 to 15 seconds after each addition.

5. Beat the mixture until it forms a dough, but do not overbeat.

6. Turn the dough out onto a floured surface and roll it out into a ¼-inch-thick circle.

7. Carefully transfer the dough to a parchment-lined baking sheet and bake for 10 to 15 minutes, until lightly browned.

8. In a mixing bowl, beat together the vegan butter spread and tofu cream cheese.

9. Add the powdered sugar in small batches, beating until smooth. Taste the mixture after 3 cups of sugar have been added and add more, if desired.

10. Beat in the almond extract and then spread the mixture evenly on the crust.

11. Arrange the sliced fruit and berries on top of the crust and chill.

12. Drizzle with maple syrup to serve, if desired.

Herb-Marinated Nectarines

SERVES 1

These nectarines are a sweet and simple dish that can be served on its own or spooned over a bowl of fresh-fruit sorbet.

¼ CUP FRESH CHOPPED MINT LEAVES

1 TABLESPOON FRESH CHOPPED BASIL LEAVES

1 TABLESPOON FRESH LEMON JUICE

1 TEASPOON PURE MAPLE SYRUP

2 RIPE NECTARINES, PITTED AND CHOPPED

CHOPPED NUTS FOR GARNISHING (OPTIONAL)

1. In a bowl, combine the mint, basil, lemon juice, and maple syrup.

2. Add the nectarines and stir well.

3. Chill for about 1 hour.

4. Serve cold, garnished with chopped nuts if desired.

Maple-Glazed Poached Pears

SERVES 2

These poached pears have enough flair to be served at a fancy dinner party, but they are also simple enough to prepare for a family meal at home.

2 RIPE PEARS, HALVED
½ CUP WATER
⅓ CUP PURE MAPLE SYRUP
1 TEASPOON VANILLA EXTRACT
1 TEASPOON ALMOND EXTRACT
PINCH OF GROUND CLOVES

1. Peel the pears, if desired, and remove the stem/core.

2. In a small saucepan, combine the remaining ingredients and bring to a boil.

3. Reduce the heat to medium-high and add the pear halves.

4. Cover the saucepan and cook for 5 to 7 minutes, until the pears are tender.

5. Remove the pears using a slotted spoon. Place the pears onto two plates.

6. Continue to simmer the glaze until thickened.

7. Drizzle the glaze over the pears to serve.

Balsamic Grilled Peaches

SERVES 4

It may not seem like fruit belongs on the grill, but after tasting this recipe, you will change your mind. The sweetness of ripe peaches is intensified by the heat of the grill, offset by the flavor of balsamic vinegar and vanilla.

½ CUP PURE MAPLE SYRUP
¼ CUP BALSAMIC VINEGAR
½ TEASPOON VANILLA EXTRACT
4 RIPE PEACHES, PITTED AND HALVED

1. In a small bowl, whisk together the maple syrup, balsamic vinegar, and vanilla extract.

2. Preheat an indoor grill pan over medium-high heat.

3. Brush half of the balsamic mixture over the peaches and place them on the grill, cut-side down.

4. Grill for about 2 minutes and then carefully flip and brush with more glaze.

5. Serve the peaches warm, drizzled with the remaining glaze.

Fresh-Fruit Freeze Pops

MAKES 8 FREEZE POPS

These pops are just what you need to cool you down on a hot day. Feel free to substitute your favorite fruit to change the flavor of these refreshing ice treats.

1 CUP WATER
½ CUP SUPERFINE SUGAR
1 TEASPOON LEMON ZEST
1 CUP SLICED STRAWBERRIES
1 CUP RASPBERRIES
1 CUP BLUEBERRIES

1. In a small saucepan, whisk together the water, sugar, and lemon zest over medium heat. Cook, stirring often, until the sugar is dissolved.

2. Remove the pan from the heat and set it aside to cool.

3. Combine the berries in a food processor and blend until pureed.

4. Stir the berries into the sugar water and then strain through a mesh sieve and discard the solids.

5. Pour the fruit liquid into ice pop molds and place in the freezer until solid.

Blueberry Sorbet

SERVES 3 TO 4

Nothing is as refreshing as a cup of cold blueberry sorbet on a hot summer's night. Made with fresh berries and lightly flavored with lemon juice, this sorbet will satisfy your sweet tooth.

½ CUP WATER
½ CUP SUPERFINE SUGAR
2 TABLESPOONS FRESH LEMON JUICE
5 CUPS BLUEBERRIES

1. In a medium saucepan, combine the water, sugar, and lemon juice over medium heat. Cook, stirring, until the sugar has dissolved.

2. Place the blueberries in a food processor and pour in the sugar mixture.

3. Blend and then strain the mixture through a mesh sieve and discard the solids.

4. Pour the blueberry syrup into a shallow dish and freeze until solid.

5. Just before serving, break the blueberry mixture into pieces and blend it in a food processor until smooth.

6. Serve immediately.

Raspberry Lime Sorbet

SERVES 5 TO 6

Raspberries are rich in vitamin C as well as a number of essential minerals. In combination with fresh lime juice, the raspberries in this sorbet provide fresh flavor as well as anti-cancer benefits.

½ CUP WATER
½ CUP SUPERFINE SUGAR
2 TABLESPOONS FRESH LIME JUICE
1 TABLESPOON LIME ZEST
5 CUPS RASPBERRIES

1. In a medium saucepan, combine the water, sugar, lime juice, and lime zest over medium heat.

2. Cook, stirring, until the sugar has dissolved. Then remove from the heat.

3. Place the raspberries in a food processor and pour in the sugar mixture.

4. Blend and then strain the mixture through a mesh sieve. Discard the solids.

5. Pour the raspberry syrup into a shallow dish and freeze until solid.

6. Just before serving, break the raspberry mixture into pieces and blend it in a food processor until smooth.

7. Serve immediately.

Raspberry "Ice Cream"

Although it can't really be called "ice cream" because it doesn't contain any cream, this dessert is cool and refreshing enough to merit the title anyway. Made with frozen bananas rather than milk or cream, this ice cream is healthy and delicious.

2 LARGE BANANAS, FROZEN
¾ CUP FROZEN RED RASPBERRIES
1 TEASPOON FRESH LEMON JUICE

1. Let the bananas and raspberries sit at room temperature for 5 to 10 minutes, until slightly defrosted.

2. Combine all of the ingredients in a food processor.

3. Blend the mixture until smooth and combined.

4. Spoon the ice cream into two dishes and serve immediately.

Whipped Coconut Cream

MAKES ABOUT 2 CUPS

Whipped coconut cream is a delicious vegan substitute for traditional whipped cream. Pipe this cream onto your favorite desserts or serve a dollop with fresh berries.

2 (8-OUNCE) CANS FULL-FAT COCONUT MILK
⅓ CUP POWDERED SUGAR

1. Chill the cans of coconut milk in the refrigerator for at least 8 hours.

2. Carefully open the cans and skim the fat from the top. Place the fat in the bowl of a stand mixer and beat for 15 to 20 seconds on low speed.

3. Add the powdered sugar and beat for 10 to 15 seconds until combined.

4. Cover the bowl and chill for about 1 hour.

5. Whip the cream by hand until smooth and serve immediately.

Whipped Chocolate Mousse

SERVES 5

This whipped chocolate mousse is just as decadent as any non-vegan dessert you have ever had. Serve it chilled topped with fresh berries or enjoy it completely on its own.

28 OUNCES SOFT REFRIGERATED TOFU
2 CUPS VEGAN CHOCOLATE OR CAROB CHIPS
1 CUP VEGAN CREAM CHEESE, ROOM TEMPERATURE
½ CUP VEGAN SOUR CREAM
1 CUP POWDERED SUGAR

1. Drain the tofu and chop it into cubes before transferring it to a food processor.

2. Blend the tofu on high speed until creamy, about 2 to 3 minutes.

3. Place the chocolate chips in a microwave-safe bowl and microwave on medium-high heat at 20-second intervals, stirring after each interval.

4. Stir the chocolate smooth when melted.

5. Drizzle it into the food processor while it is running on low speed and blend for 2 minutes until well combined.

6. Place the vegan cream cheese in the bowl of a stand mixer and beat until smooth.

7. Scrape down the sides and then add the sour cream and powdered sugar.

8. Beat the mixture on medium-high speed for about 1 minute and then beat into chocolate-tofu mixture.

9. Spoon the mousse into dessert cups.

10. Chill for 30 minutes before serving.

Most of the meat sold in grocery stores comes from animals that have never set foot on a farm. Massive corporations have replaced small farms with "factory farms," which treat animals like machines, pumping them full of antibiotics and growth hormones to make them grow quickly so they can be slaughtered and sold for human consumption.

Strawberry Chocolate Trifle

SERVES 4

This strawberry chocolate trifle is the perfectly portioned dessert for lunch or dinner parties. If you are serving buffet style, prepare the recipe in a large trifle bowl.

24 SUGARED CHOCOLATE GRAHAMS (SEE RECIPE BELOW)
½ CUP PLUS 1 TEASPOON COCONUT OIL, DIVIDED
¼ CUP EVAPORATED CANE JUICE
1 (14-OUNCE) BOX FIRM TOFU
¼ CUP UNSWEETENED COCOA POWDER
1 SMALL BOX VEGAN CHOCOLATE PUDDING MIX
½ CUP VEGAN SOUR CREAM
2 CUPS FRESH HALVED STRAWBERRIES
½ CUP VEGAN CHOCOLATE OR CAROB CHIPS

1. Break up the chocolate graham crackers by hand and place them in the food processor. Pulse until the crackers are finely crushed and then transfer them to a bowl.

2. Melt ½ cup of coconut oil and stir it into the grahams along with the cane juice. Set the mixture aside.

3. Place the tofu in a food processor and blend until smooth.

4. Blend in the cocoa powder, pudding mix, and vegan sour cream.

5. Blend the mixture on high speed for 2 minutes, until creamy and well combined.

6. Divide the graham cracker mixture between 4 dessert cups and top with alternating layers of chocolate pudding and fresh strawberries.

7. Combine the chocolate chips and remaining teaspoon of coconut oil in a microwave-safe bowl. Heat on high at 5- to 8-second intervals until melted.

8. Drizzle the melted chocolate over the trifles to serve.

Raw Coconut Fudge

SERVES ABOUT 10

The benefit of eating raw foods is that the natural enzymes in the foods are preserved. This raw coconut fudge is blended with walnuts and maple syrup to provide texture and fudge-like consistency without the need for cooking.

1¾ CUPS CHOPPED WALNUTS, DIVIDED

2 TABLESPOONS PURE MAPLE SYRUP

1 TABLESPOON WATER

2 TABLESPOONS COCONUT OIL

½ CUP UNSWEETENED SHREDDED COCONUT

2 TABLESPOONS UNSWEETENED COCOA POWDER

½ TEASPOON VANILLA EXTRACT

PINCH OF GROUND NUTMEG

1. Finely chop ¼ cup of the walnuts and set aside.

2. Place the remaining walnuts in a food processor and blend until it forms a coarse flour.

3. Transfer the flour to a bowl and stir in the remaining ingredients, including the ¼ cup of chopped walnuts.

4. Stir until the mixture is thick and well combined.

5. Pat the fudge into a dish to 1-inch thickness.

6. Cover and chill until firm (about 1 hour) and then cut into 1-inch squares.

Raw Cinnamon Raisin Cookies

These cookies are unique in that they are cooked using a dehydrator.
A dehydrator uses very low heat over extended periods of time, preserving
the natural enzymes in the food being prepared.

2 CUPS OLD-FASHIONED OATS
⅔ CUP PITTED MEDJOOL DATES
½ CUP RAISINS
½ CUP CHOPPED CASHEWS
1 TABLESPOON CINNAMON
½ TO 1 CUP UNSWEETENED APPLESAUCE

1. Place the oats in a food processor and blend until ground into a fine flour.

2. Add the dates and blend until it forms a sticky batter.

3. Transfer the batter to a mixing bowl and stir in the raisins,
cashews, and cinnamon.

4. Using your hands, blend in the applesauce about ¼ cup at a time until the
batter is pliable but holds together.

5. Shape the batter into cookies and arrange them on the trays
of your dehydrator.

6. Cook at 108°F for 8 to 12 hours.

Almond Shortbread Cookies

These almond shortbread cookies are sweet and simple. If you want a little extra sweetness, dust the cooled cookies with powdered sugar.

1 CUP COCONUT OIL
1 CUP EVAPORATED CANE JUICE
2 CUPS UNBLEACHED PASTRY FLOUR
1½ CUPS CHOPPED ALMONDS
2 TEASPOONS VANILLA EXTRACT
PINCH OF SALT

1. Preheat oven to 350°F.

2. Line a baking sheet with parchment paper.

3. In the bowl of a stand mixer, combine the coconut oil and evaporated cane juice and beat on high speed until fluffy.

4. Scrape down the sides of the bowl and then beat in the flour, almonds, vanilla extract, and salt.

5. Beat for 30 seconds and then turn the dough out onto a floured surface.

6. Knead the dough a few times, if needed, until it is well combined and stays together.

7. Shape the dough by hand into 1-inch balls and arrange them on the prepared baking sheet.

8. Bake for 10 to 12 minutes, until lightly browned and spread.

9. Leave the cookies in the pan for 2 minutes and then transfer to wire racks to cool completely before serving.

Sugared Chocolate Grahams

MAKES 24 TO 30 CRACKERS

These sugared chocolate crackers are a very versatile dessert. Serve them with fresh fruit jam or topped with chopped berries—you can even make them into dessert sandwiches, using a filling of chocolate mousse or coconut cream.

1½ CUPS WHOLE WHEAT FLOUR

½ CUP UNBLEACHED PASTRY FLOUR

½ CUP EVAPORATED CANE JUICE

⅓ CUP PLUS 1 TABLESPOON UNSWEETENED COCOA POWDER

1 TEASPOON BAKING POWDER

¼ TEASPOON SALT

4 TABLESPOONS COCONUT OIL

2 TABLESPOONS PURE MAPLE SYRUP

1 TABLESPOON DARK MOLASSES

¼ CUP WATER

¼ CUP CANE SUGAR

1. Preheat oven to 350°F.

2. Line a large baking sheet with parchment paper.

3. In the bowl of a stand mixer, combine the flours, cane juice, cocoa powder, baking powder, and salt.

4. Beat the mixture until well combined and then reduce the speed to medium and leave running.

5. Add the coconut oil 1 tablespoon at a time until it forms a crumbled mixture.

6. In a small bowl, whisk together the remaining ingredients except for the cane sugar, and beat into the flour mixture to form a smooth dough.

7. Roll the dough by hand into a ball and wrap in plastic wrap.

8. Chill the dough for 1 hour and then turn it out onto a floured surface and roll it as thin as possible.

9. Cut the dough into the desired shape and place the shapes on the prepared baking sheet.

10. Prick the crackers with the tines of a fork and sprinkle with cane sugar.

11. Bake for 12 to 15 minutes or until the crackers are just crisp.

Lemon Vanilla Cupcakes

MAKES 12 TO 14 CUPCAKES

These cupcakes are light and fluffy but full of bold lemon flavor. Frost these with your favorite icing or simply top them with a dollop of whipped coconut cream.

1½ CUPS EVAPORATED CANE JUICE

1 CUP COCONUT OIL

2 TEASPOONS VANILLA EXTRACT

2 TABLESPOONS FRESH LEMON JUICE

1 TABLESPOON FRESH LEMON ZEST

3 CUPS UNBLEACHED CAKE FLOUR

1 TABLESPOON BAKING POWDER

6 TABLESPOONS WARM WATER

1½ TABLESPOONS ENER-G EGG REPLACER

1 CUP UNSWEETENED ALMOND MILK

1 TABLESPOON DISTILLED WHITE VINEGAR

1. Preheat oven to 350°F.

2. Insert paper liners in a standard 12-cup muffin pan.

3. In the bowl of a stand mixer, combine the evaporated cane juice, coconut oil, vanilla extract, lemon juice, and lemon zest. Beat on medium speed until well combined, then scrape down the sides of the bowl.

4. Beat again on high speed for 2 minutes until fluffy.

5. In a separate bowl, whisk together the flour and baking powder.

6. In yet another bowl, combine the warm water, egg replacer, almond milk, and vinegar.

7. Beat about half of the dry ingredients into the bowl of the stand mixer and then beat in the wet ingredients.

8. Scrape down the sides of the bowl and then beat in the remainder of the dry ingredients until smooth.

9. Beat on medium speed for 30 seconds and then spoon the batter into the prepared pan, filling up each cup about ⅓ full.

10. Bake for 20 to 25 minutes, until a toothpick inserted in the center comes out clean.

11. Cool in the pan for 10 minutes before turning out onto wire racks to cool completely before frosting.

Gluten-Free Chocolate Cupcakes

MAKES ABOUT 24 CUPCAKES

Gluten-free diets have become very popular lately and though many people switch to a gluten-free diet out of medical necessity, many others do so by choice. These gluten-free chocolate cupcakes are so delicious that you will find yourself wondering why you didn't try gluten-free foods sooner.

1¾ CUPS GLUTEN-FREE ALL-PURPOSE FLOUR

¾ CUP UNSWEETENED COCOA POWDER

2 TEASPOONS BAKING SODA

1 TEASPOON BAKING POWDER

2 CUPS EVAPORATED CANE JUICE

2 CUPS UNSWEETENED ALMOND MILK

½ CUP MELTED COCONUT OIL

1 TABLESPOON DISTILLED WHITE VINEGAR

1 TEASPOON VANILLA EXTRACT

4 TABLESPOONS WARM WATER

1 TABLESPOON ENER-G EGG REPLACER

1. Preheat oven to 350°F.

2. Insert paper liners in 2 standard 12-cup muffin pans..

3. In the bowl of a stand mixer, combine the flour, cocoa, baking soda, and baking powder. Beat in the cane juice.

4. In another bowl, whisk together the almond milk, coconut oil, vinegar, and vanilla extract.

5. With the stand mixer running on low speed, pour in the almond milk mixture and beat for 30 seconds, until smooth.

6. In a small bowl, whisk together the warm water and egg replacer.

7. Add the egg replacer to the bowl of the stand mixer and beat for another 30 seconds.

8. Spoon the batter into the prepared pans, filling each cup with $\frac{1}{4}$ cup batter.

9. Bake for 18 to 20 minutes, until a toothpick inserted in the center comes out clean.

10. Cool in the pans for 30 minutes before frosting.

Cinnamon Carrot Cake

SERVES 8 TO 10

Carrot cake is a classic dessert and one that you can still enjoy while following a vegan diet. By substituting canola oil or applesauce for butter, you can make virtually any cake recipe vegan friendly.

COOKING SPRAY

2½ CUPS UNBLEACHED PASTRY FLOUR,
    PLUS EXTRA TO FLOUR CAKE PANS

2 CUPS EVAPORATED CANE JUICE

1¾ TEASPOONS BAKING POWDER

1¼ TEASPOONS BAKING SODA

¾ TEASPOON SALT

1 TABLESPOON GROUND CINNAMON

¾ CUP UNSWEETENED COCONUT FLAKES

1½ CUPS CHOPPED WALNUTS, DIVIDED

4 TABLESPOONS WARM WATER

1 TABLESPOON ENER-G EGG REPLACER

1 CUP CANOLA OIL

1 CUP UNSWEETENED APPLESAUCE

1 TEASPOON VANILLA EXTRACT

2 CUPS SHREDDED CARROTS

VEGAN CREAM CHEESE FROSTING

1. Preheat oven to 350°F.

2. Lightly oil and flour two round 9-inch cake pans.

3. Using a stand mixer, beat together the pastry flour, cane juice, baking powder, baking soda, salt, and ground cinnamon.

4. Add the coconut and ½ cup chopped walnuts and blend well.

5. In a small bowl, whisk together the warm water and Ener-g Egg Replacer.

6. Beat in the canola oil, applesauce, and vanilla extract into the stand mixer bowl, and then beat in the egg replacer.

7. Fold in the shredded carrots.

8. Divide the batter evenly between the two prepared pans and bake for 30 to 35 minutes, until a knife inserted in the center comes out clean.

9. Allow the cake to cool for 10 minutes and then turn out onto wire racks to cool completely before frosting.

Red Velvet Cake

SERVES 8 TO 10

This red velvet cake looks just as good as it tastes. Frost it with vegan cream cheese icing and sprinkle with red sugar for a delectable dessert on date night.

COOKING SPRAY
2 CUPS EVAPORATED CANE JUICE
⅔ CUP VEGAN BUTTER SUBSTITUTE
2½ TABLESPOONS UNSWEETENED COCOA POWDER
¾ TEASPOON SALT
2 TEASPOONS BAKING SODA
6 TABLESPOONS WARM WATER
1½ TABLESPOONS ENER-G EGG REPLACER
1½ CUPS UNSWEETENED ALMOND MILK
2 TABLESPOONS DISTILLED WHITE VINEGAR
1 TEASPOON ALMOND EXTRACT
1 TEASPOON VANILLA EXTRACT
3 TABLESPOONS ALL-NATURAL RED FOOD COLORING
3½ CUPS UNBLEACHED PASTRY FLOUR, PLUS EXTRA TO FLOUR PANS
VEGAN CREAM CHEESE FROSTING

1. Preheat oven to 350°F.

2. Lightly oil and flour two round 9-inch cake pans.

3. In the bowl of a stand mixer, beat together the cane juice, butter substitute, cocoa powder, salt, and baking soda for about 2 minutes.

4. In another bowl, whisk together the warm water and egg replacer.

5. Whisk the almond milk into the egg replacer, along with the vinegar, extracts, and food coloring.

6. Keep the stand mixer running on low speed as you pour in the wet ingredients and the pastry flour in alternating batches.

7. Beat until the batter is smooth and then divide evenly between the two prepared pans.

8. Bake for 25 to 30 minutes, until a knife inserted in the center comes out clean.

9. Cool in the pans for 10 minutes and then turn out onto wire racks to cool completely before frosting.

Fruit and Nut Granola Bars

MAKES ABOUT 12 BARS

If you are looking for a healthy snack to serve your children, these fruit and nut granola bars are packed with protein and dietary fiber, not to mention delicious flavor.

COOKING SPRAY

1½ CUPS OLD-FASHIONED ROLLED OATS

2 TABLESPOONS CANOLA OIL

1 TABLESPOON MELTED COCONUT OIL

PINCH OF SALT

¼ CUP LIGHT BROWN SUGAR, PACKED

¼ CUP PURE MAPLE SYRUP

1½ TEASPOONS ALMOND EXTRACT

½ CUP FLAXSEED MEAL OR WHEAT GERM

¼ CUP DRIED CRANBERRIES OR RAISINS

¼ CUP CHOPPED PECANS

¼ CUP CHOPPED WALNUTS

1. Preheat oven to 350°F.

2. Lightly oil an 8 x 8-inch glass baking dish.

3. In a medium bowl, stir together the old-fashioned oats, canola oil, coconut oil, and salt.

4. Spread the oat mixture out evenly on a rimmed baking sheet.

5. Bake for 15 to 18 minutes, until the oats are lightly toasted.

6. Reduce oven temperature to 325°F.

7. In a small saucepan, combine the brown sugar and maple syrup over medium heat.

8. Heat until the brown sugar is dissolved and the mixture is hot.

9. Whisk the mixture smooth and then remove from heat and whisk in the almond extract.

10. In a large bowl, combine the remaining ingredients, including the toasted oats, and stir in the maple syrup mixture until well combined.

11. Transfer the mixture to the prepared baking dish and press it down evenly.

12. Bake for 20 to 25 minutes, until the edges are lightly browned.

13. Cool for 15 to 20 minutes before cutting.

Cinnamon Raisin Oatmeal Bars

MAKES ABOUT 12 BARS

Oats are an excellent source of dietary fiber. And when combined with the flavors of cinnamon and raisins, they make for a tasty snack bar.

COOKING SPRAY

¾ CUP UNSWEETENED APPLESAUCE

½ CUP LIGHT BROWN SUGAR, PACKED

1 TEASPOON VANILLA EXTRACT

1 CUP OLD-FASHIONED ROLLED OATS

1 CUP WHITE RICE FLOUR

1 TEASPOON BAKING POWDER

1½ TEASPOONS CINNAMON

½ CUP UNSWEETENED COCONUT MILK

½ CUP RAISINS

1. Preheat oven to 350°F.

2. Lightly oil an 8 x 8-inch square glass baking dish.

3. In a medium bowl, combine the applesauce, brown sugar, and vanilla, and whisk until smooth and combined.

4. In a separate bowl, combine the oats, rice flour, baking powder, and cinnamon, and stir the mixture into the applesauce-brown sugar mixture.

5. Whisk in the coconut milk in a steady stream, stirring until the mixture forms a smooth dough.

6. Fold in the raisins and transfer the dough to the prepared baking dish.

7. Bake for 18 to 22 minutes, until the edges are lightly browned.

8. Cool the bars completely before serving.

Chocolate Peanut Butter Bars

MAKES 16 BARS

Peanut butter and chocolate is a match made in heaven. If you aren't already a believer, this recipe might convert you. Try this recipe after making a batch of Sugared Chocolate Grahams.

2 CUPS POWDERED SUGAR

1½ CUPS CRUSHED SUGARED CHOCOLATE GRAHAMS
   (SEE PAGE 208)

1 CUP ALL-NATURAL SMOOTH PEANUT BUTTER

½ CUP PLUS 6 TABLESPOONS COCONUT OIL, DIVIDED

3 TABLESPOONS WATER

1 CUP VEGAN CHOCOLATE CHIPS OR CAROB CHIPS

1. In the bowl of a stand mixer, combine the powdered sugar and crushed graham crackers.

2. Beat in the peanut butter, ½ cup coconut oil, and water until the mixture is smooth and creamy.

3. Line an 8 × 8-inch baking dish with foil and spread the peanut butter mixture evenly along the bottom of it.

4. Combine the remaining coconut oil with the chocolate chips in a double boiler over medium-low heat.

5. Heat the mixture until melted, then stir smooth.

6. Spread the chocolate over the peanut butter layer as evenly as possible.

7. Chill for 1 hour.

8. Cut into 2-inch squares to serve.

Chocolate Peanut Butter Rice Bars

MAKES ABOUT 18 BARS

Pack one of these into your child's lunch or keep the bars on hand for an afternoon snack. These treats are quick to make and sure to satisfy your snack cravings.

COOKING SPRAY

8 CUPS BROWN RICE CEREAL

¼ CUP FLAXSEED MEAL

2 TABLESPOONS UNSWEETENED COCOA POWDER

1 CUP BROWN RICE SYRUP

½ CUP PEANUT BUTTER

¾ TEASPOON VANILLA EXTRACT

1. Lightly oil a 9 × 13-inch glass baking dish with cooking spray and set aside.

2. In a large bowl, stir together the brown rice cereal, flaxseed, and cocoa powder.

3. In a small pan, combine the brown rice syrup, peanut butter, and vanilla extract over medium heat.

4. Heat the mixture, stirring occasionally, until smooth and melted, about 5 minutes.

5. Pour the melted syrup mixture into the bowl with the cereal and stir well until it is completely incorporated.

6. Press the cereal mixture into the baking dish and pat it down evenly by hand.

7. Cover and chill for 1 hour before cutting.

Spiced Pumpkin Bars

MAKES 8 TO 10 BARS

These bars are the perfect snack if you find yourself craving something sweet. Made with pumpkin and oats, these are rich in dietary fiber as well as delicious taste.

COOKING SPRAY
1 CUP PUMPKIN PUREE
½ CUP LIGHT BROWN SUGAR, PACKED
1 TEASPOON VANILLA EXTRACT
1 CUP OLD-FASHIONED ROLLED OATS
1 CUP UNBLEACHED ALL-PURPOSE FLOUR (OR WHITE RICE FLOUR)
1½ TEASPOONS PUMPKIN PIE SPICE
1 TEASPOON BAKING POWDER
½ CUP UNSWEETENED COCONUT MILK

1. Preheat oven to 350°F.

2. Lightly oil a square 8 × 8-inch glass dish.

3. Combine the pumpkin puree and brown sugar in a medium bowl and beat on medium speed with a hand mixer until fluffy.

4. Beat in the vanilla extract and then set aside.

5. In a separate bowl, stir together the oats, flour, pumpkin pie spice, and baking powder.

6. Fold the oat mixture into the pumpkin-puree mixture.

7. Whisk in the milk, pouring it in a steady stream, and beat until a smooth dough forms in the bowl.

8. Transfer the dough to the prepared dish and bat it down evenly.

9. Bake for 18 to 22 minutes, until the dough is lightly browned on the edges.

10. Set the dish aside to cool completely before serving.

Hot-and-Salty Mixed Nuts

MAKES ABOUT 2½ CUPS

These mixed nuts are the ideal finger food to serve at your next house party. Not only are they full of protein and healthy fats, but nuts are also a flavorful snack.

3 TABLESPOONS COCONUT OIL

1 TABLESPOON PURE MAPLE SYRUP

½ TEASPOON WASABI PASTE

1 TEASPOON SALT, DIVIDED

¾ CUP RAW CASHEWS

½ CUP WALNUT HALVES

½ CUP RAW ALMONDS

¼ CUP RAW PECAN HALVES

¼ TEASPOON CAYENNE PEPPER

1. Preheat oven to 300°F.

2. Line a baking sheet with parchment paper.

3. In a small saucepan, whisk together the coconut oil, maple syrup, wasabi paste, and ½ teaspoon of the salt over medium-low heat. Cook until smooth and melted, stirring as needed.

4. In a medium bowl, combine the nuts and then pour the coconut-oil mixture over them, tossing well to coat.

5. Spread the nuts on the prepared baking sheet and bake for 15 to 20 minutes until lightly toasted.

6. Allow the nuts to cool.

7. Place them in a bowl and sprinkle with cayenne pepper and the remaining salt. Toss to coat, and serve.

Sweet-and-Salty Trail Mix

MAKES ABOUT 3 CUPS

Trail mix is the perfect on-the-go snack. Simply portion it out into bags or small plastic containers, and toss it into your lunch bag for later.

3 TABLESPOONS EXTRA-VIRGIN OLIVE OIL

2 TABLESPOONS PURE MAPLE SYRUP

1¼ TEASPOONS SALT, DIVIDED

½ CUP RAW CASHEW HALVES

½ CUP RAW WALNUT HALVES

½ CUP RAW ALMONDS

¼ CUP SHELLED PISTACHIOS

¼ CUP DRIED CRANBERRIES

¼ CUP GOLDEN RAISINS

1. Preheat oven to 300°F.

2. Line a baking sheet with parchment paper.

3. In a small saucepan, whisk together the olive oil, maple syrup, and 1 teaspoon of the salt over medium-low heat.

4. Stir the mixture until it is melted and smooth and then remove from the heat.

5. In a medium bowl, combine the cashews, walnuts, almonds, and pistachios and pour the olive-oil mixture over them.

6. Toss to coat the nuts, and then spread them on the prepared baking sheet.

7. Bake for 15 to 20 minutes, until lightly toasted, and then cool for 10 minutes.

8. Transfer the nuts to a bowl and add the cranberries and raisins.

9. Toss the mixture with the remaining ¼ teaspoon of salt and serve.

Baked Sweet Potato Chips

SERVES 3 TO 4

Not all chips are greasy and fattening. In fact, these sweet potato chips are baked, not fried, which gives them that delicious crunch without all the extra oil.

2 LARGE SWEET POTATOES
1½ TABLESPOONS EXTRA-VIRGIN OLIVE OIL
SALT TO TASTE
FRESHLY GROUND BLACK PEPPER TO TASTE

1. Preheat oven to 200°F.

2. Rinse the potatoes and pat them dry with paper towel.

3. Slice the sweet potatoes as thinly as possible and place them in a medium bowl.

4. Add the olive oil, salt, and pepper and toss to coat the sliced sweet potatoes.

5. Arrange the sweet potato slices in a single layer on baking sheets and bake for about 45 minutes.

6. Flip the potato slices and bake for another 35 to 45 minutes, until the slices are crisp.

7. Cool slightly and serve warm.

Sugared Apple Chips

SERVES 3

These sugared apple chips are the perfect blend of sweet and tart. Enjoy them on their own or as a garnish for your favorite dessert or salad.

3 RIPE APPLES
½ CUP POWDERED SUGAR
PINCH OF GROUND CINNAMON

1. Preheat oven to 250°F.

2. Line a baking sheet with parchment paper.

3. Core and thinly slice the apples.

4. In a medium bowl, whisk together the powdered sugar and cinnamon and then dip the apple slices in the mixture.

5. Arrange the slices on the prepared baking sheet and bake for 20 to 25 minutes, until the apples are lightly browned and crisp.

6. Store the chips in an airtight container once they are cooled.

. . . .

Just because potato chips and candy bars might be vegetarian doesn't mean they should become a staple of your diet. The key to a healthy vegetarian diet is achieving a balance of nutrients with a variety of fruits, vegetables, and vegetarian protein sources.

. . . .

Cinnamon Baked Apple Chips

SERVES 3 TO 4

These apple chips are great as a snack, appetizer, or dessert. Full of fresh apple flavor and baked to perfection, these are something you will always want to have on hand.

4 RIPE GALA APPLES
1 TABLESPOON GROUND CINNAMON
1 TEASPOON CANE SUGAR

1. Preheat oven to 325°F.

2. Line a standard baking sheet with parchment paper.

3. Rinse the apples and remove the cores. Slice the apples as thinly as possible and then place them in a medium mixing bowl.

4. Add the cinnamon and sugar and toss to coat the apples.

5. Arrange the apple slices on the baking sheet and bake for 30 minutes.

6. Carefully flip the slices and bake for another 35 to 45 minutes, until the moisture has baked out.

7. Turn off the oven and let the apple chips sit until crisp.

8. Store in an airtight container.

Sesame Kale Chips

SERVES 3 TO 4

Though kale is traditionally served steamed or in a salad, it also makes a wonderfully crisp chip. These sesame kale chips are incredibly simple to make and they are just as nutritious as they are delicious.

1 BUNCH FRESH KALE LEAVES
1 TABLESPOON OLIVE OIL
1 TEASPOON RAW SESAME SEEDS

1. Preheat oven to 350°F.

2. Rinse the kale in fresh water and then pat dry with paper towels.

3. Tear the kale leaves into 2-inch chunks and place them in a bowl.

4. Add the olive oil and sesame seeds and toss to coat.

5. Arrange the kale on a baking sheet and bake for 15 to 20 minutes, until the leaves are crisp. Serve immediately.

Conclusion

After reading this book, you may find yourself wondering why you didn't make the switch to a vegan lifestyle sooner.

You do not have to be a fanatical animal rights activist to follow a vegan lifestyle. In fact, you might make the switch simply out of a desire to improve your health and to reduce your risk for chronic disease. Whatever your motivation may be, know that going vegan is always a good choice. Hopefully, the information in this book will help you succeed in making the transition and in living a healthy and fulfilling vegan life.

Glossary

Albumin: a globular protein found in milk and eggs; often used in cosmetics as a coagulating agent and in baked goods.

Antioxidants: molecules that prevent other molecules from oxidizing. Protect cells from free radical damage and may also help prevent cancer and other chronic diseases.

Atherosclerosis: a condition characterized by the thickening of artery walls as a result of the accumulation of cholesterol and other fatty materials.

Blender: commonly referred to as a liquidizer in the United Kingdom; an electrical appliance used to puree or emulsify foods.

Casein: a type of protein found in milk; often used as an additive in cheeses, non-dairy creamers, and cosmetics.

Dehydrator: an appliance that uses heat and airflow to remove moisture from food.

Detoxification: the removal of a harmful substance, such as a poison or toxin, or the effect of such.

Dietary Vegan: an individual who follows a vegan lifestyle in order to live a healthy life.

Environmental Vegan: an individual who follows a vegan lifestyle out of concern for sustainability and other environmental issues.

Ethical Vegan: an individual who follows a vegan lifestyle for ethical reasons based on the idea that all sentient beings have the right to live lives free from suffering at the hands of humans.

Food Processor: a kitchen appliance that can be used to peel, chop, or puree foods.

Gelatin: a colorless, flavorless substance derived from animal byproducts, often used as a thickener in candies and puddings. Produced by boiling in water the skin, tendons, ligaments, and bones of slaughtered livestock.

Ghee: a type of clarified butter commonly used in South Asian cuisine.

Juicer: a kitchen appliance that extracts the juice from fresh fruits and vegetables by various means. Three types: centrifugal, mastication and triturating.

Lactose: a type of sugar derived from the glucose and galactose in milk.

Phytochemicals or phytonutrients: compounds that naturally occur in plants and have biological significance (i.e., antioxidants).

Seitan: a meat substitute made from wheat; an excellent source of vegetarian protein.

Tempeh: a meat substitute made from fermented soy beans and rice; a good source of vegetarian protein and dietary fiber.

Tofu: also called bean curd; made by coagulating soy milk and pressing the curd into blocks.

Vegan: an individual who practices veganism; may also apply to foods that meet the standards of a vegan diet.

Vegan Society: a society founded in 1944 in England to promote awareness of the vegan lifestyle and to provide support for those who follow it.

Veganism: the practice of abstaining from the use and consumption of animal products.

Vegetarian: an individual who abstains from the consumption of meat and seafood; some vegetarians still consume eggs, milk, and other dairy products.

References
and Resources

Anderson, Kathleen. "Excess Iron and Brain Degeneration: The Little-Known Link." LEF.org: Live Extension Magazine. <http://www.lef.org/magazine/mag2012/mar2012_Excess-Iron-Brain-Degeneration_01.htm>

Barnard, Neal D., et al. "The Medical Costs Attributable to Meat Consumption." *Preventive Medicine* 24, 646-655 (1995). <http://birdflubook.com/resources/Barnard_1995_PM_24_646.pdf>

Bartzokis, et al. "Premenopausal Hysterectomy is Associated with Increased Brain Ferritin Iron." *Neurobiological Aging.* 2012 Sept; 33 (9): 1950-8. 2011. <http://www.ncbi.nlm.nih.gov/pubmed/21925770>

Charity Commission Registered Charity no. 279228, The Vegan Society <http://apps.charitycommission.gov.uk/Showcharity/RegisterOfCharities/Charity-WithoutPartB.aspx?RegisteredCharityNumber=279228&SubsidiaryNumber=0>

Dai, Q., et al. "Fruit and Vegetable Juices and Alzheimer's Disease: the Kame Project." *American Journal of Medicine.* 2006 Sept; 119 (9): 751-9. <http://www.ncbi.nlm.nih.gov/pubmed/16945610>

"Dietary Reference Intakes (DRIs): Estimated Average Requirements." National Academy of Sciences Institute of Medicine Food and Nutrition Board. <http://www.iom.edu/Activities/Nutrition/SummaryDRIs/~/media/Files/Activity%20Files/Nutrition/DRIs/5_Summary%20Table%20Tables%201-4.pdf>

Marmot, Michael, et al. "Food, Nutrition, Physical Activity and the Prevention of Cancer: A Global Perspective." Published by the American Institute for Cancer Research and the World Cancer Research Fund. (2007). <http://eprints.ucl.ac.uk/4841/1/4841.pdf>

Meat Consumption and Cancer Risk. The Physicians Committee for Responsible Medicine (PCRM). <http://pcrm.org/search/?cid=3542>

Murphy, Andrew J., et al. "Cholesterol Efflux in Megakaryocyte Progenitors Suppresses Platelet Production and Thrombocytosis." *Nature Medicine.* 19, 586-594 (2013). <http://www.nature.com/nm/journal/v19/n5/abs/nm.3150.html>

Pan, An, et al. "Changes in Red Meat Consumption and Subsequent Risk of Type 2 Diabetes Mellitus." *The Journal of the American Medical Association; Internal Medicine.* 2013, published online. <http://archinte.jamanetwork.com/article.aspx?articleid=1697785#AuthorInformation>

Rouse, et al. "Vegetarian Diet, Lifestyle and Blood Pressure in Two Religious Populations." *Journal of Clinical and Experimental Pharmacology and Physiology.* 1982 May-Jun; 9 (3): 327-30. <http://www.ncbi.nlm.nih.gov/pubmed/7140012>

Sellmeyer, Deborah E., et al. "A High Ratio of Dietary Animal to Vegetable Protein Increases the Rate of Bone Loss and the Risk of Fracture in Postmenopausal Women." *The American Journal of Clinical Nutrition.* Jan 2001: 73 (1); 118-122. < http://ajcn.nutrition.org/content/73/1/118.full>

Tantamango-Bartley, Y., et al. "Vegetarian Diets and the Incidence of Cancer in a Low-Risk Population." *Cancer Epidemiology Biomarkers and Prevention.* 2013 Feb: 22 (2): 286-94. < http://www.ncbi.nlm.nih.gov/pubmed/23169929>
Tucker, K.L., et al. "The Acid-Base Hypothesis: Diet and Bone in the Framingham Osteoporosis Study." *European Journal of Nutrition.* 2001 Oct; 40 (5): 231-7. < http://www.ncbi.nlm.nih.gov/pubmed/11842948>

Wang, Y and Beydoun MA. "Meat Consumption is Associated with Obesity and Central Obesity Among US Adults." *The International Journal of Obesity.* 2009 June; 33(6):621-8. < http://www.ncbi.nlm.nih.gov/pubmed/19308071>

Index

Printed in Great Britain
by Amazon